no-fuss suppers

no-fuss suppers

deliciously simple recipes for cooking after work

Caroline Marson photography by Peter Cassidy

RYLAND
PETERS
& SMALL

LONDON NEW YORK

Dedication

For Simon, Freddie and Daisy...

Author's acknowledgements

Thanks goes to my wise mother who was a spot-on guinea pig and put up with her kitchen being wrecked for a week. Thanks to my father for his creative thinking and encouragement. Thanks also to my lovely husband Simon who spent ages gazing into the fridge wondering what combination he was allowed to eat and what he had to keep his hands off! Thanks to my son Freddie for continuously making me laugh and for creating delightful concoctions in a vain hope that they might make the book. A huge thank you also goes to all at Ryland Peters & Small – especially Alison Starling, Julia Charles and Steve Painter – and to photographer Peter Cassidy and food stylist Tonia George. And finally, a big thank you to all my girlfriends who helped me with the school run, entertained my son and walked my dog Daisy.

First published in the United Kingdom in 2006
by Ryland Peters & Small
20–21 Jockey's Fields
London WC1R 4BW
www.rylandpeters.com

10 9 8 7 6 5 4 3 2 1

Text © Caroline Marson 2006
Design and photographs
© Ryland Peters & Small 2006

ISBN-10: 1 84597 211 2
ISBN-13: 978 1 84597 211 0

A catalogue record for this book is available from the British Library.

Printed and bound in China.

Design and photographic art direction Steve Painter
Commissioning Editor Julia Charles
Production Gordana Simakovic
Art Director Anne-Marie Bulat
Publishing Director Alison Starling

Food Stylist Tonia George
Prop Stylist Liz Belton
Indexer Hilary Bird

Notes

• All spoon measurements are level unless otherwise stated.

• Eggs are UK large size unless specified otherwise. Uncooked or partially cooked eggs should not be served to the very old, frail, young children, pregnant women or those with compromised immune systems.

contents

introduction

This book is for busy people with hectic lives who enjoy good food but have little or no time to cook. Whether you have a long commute to and from work each day, or juggle school runs with part-time work, the chances are you live your life in the fast lane. Perhaps understandably, taking time to cook a fresh meal from scratch is often low on the list of priorities. Ready-meals and take-aways seem like a good solution for the time-poor, but they are not the answer. They are often high in salt, fat and artificial additives, and low in taste. And, quite simply, there is no pleasure to be had from putting a ready-meal in the microwave – it is a short-term fix with no heart or soul. Cooking is a pleasurable and therapeutic pastime, and the ideal way to unwind after a long and demanding day.

In *No-fuss Suppers* I will show you how to make the most of good, fresh ingredients and help you understand that by keeping things simple, it's possible to look forward to an imaginative evening meal without dreading the cooking during the day. I use ingredients that are available in most supermarkets and have made the methods of cooking as short and straightforward as possible. The recipes are all suitable for beginners and more experienced cooks alike, and include No-cook Deli Suppers (imaginative ideas for quickly assembled pizzas, pastas, platters and salads), Simple Suppers for every day, Light Bites for when soup or a salad is all you fancy, Supper for Friends for slightly more sophisticated evenings and a selection of delicious treats in Sweet Things. Finally, in Transforming Simple Food I show you how creative use of pestos, butters, marinades, rubs and dressings can turn a simple meal into something really special.

All of these recipes should not take longer than 30 minutes to prepare from start to finish and some take even less time or need no cooking at all. Most of the recipes serve two people because that's how many of us live these days, but halve or double up as you need to. Make sure you have got a good array of different sized, heavy-based pots and pans. Additionally, good-quality knives, kept razor sharp and safely put away in a knife block, are a must.

Easy steps to No-fuss Suppers:

★ Begin by planning for when you are likely to be in or out during the weeks ahead and shop accordingly. This common-sense approach will mean you can buy foods specifically for each night rather than randomly buying foods that will not be used. Make a list and stick to it – don't be tempted to impulse buy.

★ Shop weekly for fresh fruit and vegetables or use an organic box delivery service. Choose seasonal foods where possible as they will last longer and taste better.

★ Become a regular at your local deli or supermarket deli counter and buy semi-prepared ingredients for super-fast suppers.

★ Stock up on storecupboard essentials such as spices, sauces and flavourings that will add depth and flavour to basic food (see pages 8–9).

★ Fill your freezer with bags of convenient frozen fresh foods such as vegetables, fish and seafood, mixed berries and packets of chopped fresh herbs (see page 9). Double up when cooking and freeze extra servings to enjoy on another evening. Make sure you always have plenty of freezer bags and freezer-proof airtight plastic containers to hand.

★ Prepare ahead – many dishes can be part-assembled in the morning or even the night before and stored in the fridge until needed. Also, if you are chopping onions or garlic for today's supper, chop a little extra for tomorrow. These ingredients will stay fresh in the fridge for up to 4 days if stored in sealed containers.

I hope you will be inspired by these simple recipes. The ingredients and methods suggested are not cast in stone; they are flexible and designed to encourage you to be creative, so do experiment and tweak them to suit your own taste as you go along. Discover your own favourites and wave goodbye to ready-meals once and for all!

storecupboard essentials

It's a good idea to keep your storecupboard, fridge and freezer well stocked with useful ingredients – you'll always be able to produce a quick supper, even if you've not had time to buy anything in. Any additional fresh food should be bought often and in small quantities so that it is always the freshest it can be.

Staples

You will never be far from a meal if you have these key staple ingredients ready and waiting in your kitchen cupboards.

★ **Dried pasta** – make sure it is durum wheat or semolina pasta. Keep a good selection of shapes from penne or rigatoni to spaghetti or tagliatelle.

★ **Rice** – long-grain, basmati, Thai or jasmine fragrant and microwavable rice; Arborio for risottos.

★ **Egg or rice noodles** – look for 'straight-to-wok' brands for stir-fries.

★ **Couscous** – great for spicy dishes. Just needs plumping up in hot water or stock.

★ **Pizza bases** – either long-life or frozen.

★ **Beans** – tins of cooked, mixed beans, such as kidney, cannellini and butter beans, and chickpeas.

★ **Crab meat** – tins of crab meat are handy for making fishcakes and adding to salads.

★ **Tinned chopped tomatoes** – either plain or seasoned with mixed herbs or garlic. Great for instant pizza base sauce.

★ **Passata** – indispensible puréed and sieved tomatoes that can be made into soup, used as a pizza topping or made into a pasta sauce.

★ **Tuna flakes** – tinned or in jars with olive oil for salads.

★ **Coconut milk** – for Thai curries and soups.

★ **Toasted nuts** – pine nuts, almonds, hazelnuts etc., stored in airtight containers.

★ **Pumpkin and sunflower seeds** – useful for snacking and sprinkling on salads.

★ **Pitted black and green olives** – keep tins and jars of olives, either plain or marinated.

★ **Capers** – small capers and large caper berries.

★ **Porridge oats** – for making flapjacks and puddings. Choose the organic, jumbo variety.

Flavour enhancers

Add these seasonings only after you have tasted the food. A pinch or a drop will add 'high' or 'low' tones to your cooking.

★ **Sea salt flakes** and **freshly ground black pepper** – essential seasoning.

★ **Dark and light soy sauce** – for adding salt to oriental dishes.

★ **Thai fish sauce (nam pla)** – add to all Thai food for that instant authentic flavour.

★ **Lemon and lime juice** – use instead of salt for adding 'high' tones.

★ **Balsamic vinegar** – syrupy balsamic vinegar. Put in a spray bottle and spritz onto salads.

★ **Vinegars** – cider, white wine, red wine and tarragon for dressings.

★ **Mustards** – Dijon, wholegrain and English.

★ **Anchovy paste or fillets** – a paste or essence with a long fridge life. Great for adding flavour.

★ **Tomato purée** – adds depth to tomato sauces.

★ **Pomegranate molasses** – a thick sweet syrup good for dressings.

★ **Marmite** – great for making gravies like your grandma's and for spreading on toast 'soldiers'.

★ **Marigold Swiss vegetable bouillon** – better than stock cubes. Add a pinch when cooking rice.

Oils

Using the right oil can make or break a dish – consider how much flavour you want to add when deciding which to use.

★ **Light olive oil** – for cooking and **extra virgin olive oil** for drizzling onto salads. Flavour a bottle of good olive oil with sprigs of tarragon and garlic.

★ **Sunflower or groundnut oil** – for pan-frying and stirfrying.

★ **Walnut or hazelnut oil** – use in tiny amounts to add a nutty flavour to salad dressings.

★ **Sesame oil** – for seasoning Asian wok dishes – add at the end of cooking for a finishing flavour.

Seasonings and spices

These will add character to your cooking. Use in small quantities and make sure they are cooked well for a smoother flavour.

★ **Fresh ginger root** – grate into, or add shavings to, oriental stir-fries and curries. Also good with ham.

★ **Red chillies** – the membranes and seeds hold most of the hotness, so remove if you don't want to add heat. The longer they are cooked, the hotter the dish will become.

★ **Lemongrass** – remove the outer leaves and simply chop the tender leaves and add to Thai stir-fries or curries.

★ **Garlic** – ideally a fresh bulb, but a tube or jar of garlic purée can be useful.

★ **Crushed dried chillies** – add a powerful instant heat to a wide variety of dishes. Sprinkle onto steaks and fish.

★ **Saffron threads or powder** – add to marinades or mayonnaise. Use sparingly as a little goes a long way, or steep a pinch in hot water before adding.

★ **Sichuan peppercorns** – not from the same family as black peppercorns. Crush them and use to coat chicken or duck breasts before cooking.

★ **Whole and ground cumin and coriander** – these two spices go hand in hand and are good for giving a dish a North African flavour. Gently roast to release their flavour before adding.

★ **Turmeric** – adds brilliant yellow colour and an earthy flavour to Indian curries, rice and vegetables.

★ **Ground cinnamon and cinnamon sticks** – warming spice good for savoury or fruit desserts. Stir hot chocolate with a cinnamon stick.

★ **Pimentón (Spanish oak-smoked paprika)** – spice used in chorizo sausage, good for Tex-mex flavour and barbecue sauces.

★ **Cardamom** – the outer green pod is not eaten. Use in a warm fruit salad to add aromatic spice.

★ **Cayenne pepper** – this fiery spice adds flavour to dips and marinades.

★ **Garam masala** – added to Indian curries, towards the end of cooking, for extra flavour.

★ **Chinese five-spice** – this wonder powder will enliven bland dishes from stir-fries to marinades.

Magic jars

These pastes, chutneys, sauces and ketchups are a godsend for bringing variety and flair to your weekday cooking.

★ **Sweet chilli sauce** – a sweet, fruity sauce. Add fresh coriander and use as an instant dip for prawn crackers.

★ **Hoisin sauce** – for Chinese pancakes or barbecued ribs and chicken.

★ **Plum sauce** – made from plums, apricots and vinegar. Add to pork stir-fries or use as a marinade for chicken breasts.

★ **Good-quality mayonnaise** – good for quick dips and salad dressings.

★ **Tom yum paste** – hot and sour paste. An ideal base for making exquisite instant Thai soup.

★ **Madras curry paste** – a sweet tangy base for an authentic South Indian curry.

★ **Mint sauce** – if you don't have fresh mint, use this for marinating lamb steaks or chops.

★ **Horseradish sauce** – add to crème fraîche and spread onto roast beef sandwiches.

★ **Wasabi** – mix with soft butter and serve a dollop on grilled steak or salmon.

★ **Mango chutney** – adds zip to grilled chicken. As well as curry, it's great with cheese and biscuits.

★ **Jalapeño chillies** – very hot, lovely chopped and added to a tub of ready-made guacamole. Avoid touching your face when handling them!

★ **Olive and artichoke tapenades** – spread on hot toast, bruschetta or oat cakes for a snack.

★ **Tabasco sauce** – add a dash to a tin of chopped tomatoes with spring onions and fresh coriander for an instant tomato salsa. Adds zest to numerous dishes.

★ **Worcestershire sauce** – add to gravies, sausages and cheese-on-toast.

★ **Tomato ketchup** – a good addition to barbecue sauces, bacon sandwiches and Bolognese sauce.

★ **Thai curry paste** – use red or green for a speedy Thai curry or soup.

Sweet things

Your sweet cravings can be satisfied at a moment's notice with some of my favourite handy storecupboard standbys.

★ **75% cocoa solids dark chocolate and good-quality white chocolate** – buy the best for chocolate sauce and snacking.

★ **Good-quality cocoa powder** – tastes bitter, but gives a deep chocolate flavour to puddings and brownies. Use for dusting over desserts.

★ **Jars of fruit compote** – for instant fruit fools and sauces, and adding to yoghurt and ice cream.

★ **Orange flower water** – for sprinkling onto fruit salads.

★ **Stem ginger in syrup** – add to whipped cream, ice cream, chocolate and biscuits.

★ **Good-quality lemon curd** – mix with cream and use as a topping for shortbread or scones.

★ **Organic and dried prunes, pears and apricots** – for tea-soaked fruits served with ice cream.

★ **Dried cranberries and cherries** – for sprinkling onto fruit tarts or stirring into plain yoghurt.

★ **Biscotti or cantucci** – crisp Italian biscuits for dunking into dessert wine or serving with coffee.

★ **Sponge fingers (savordi)** – for making tiramisu or trifle.

★ **Amaretti or ratafia biscuits** – soaked in sherry, they can be used as a base for trifle.

★ **Runny or thick honey** – for drizzling onto toast and stirring into Greek yoghurt.

★ **Sugar** – muscovado for a caramel taste; caster, granulated and icing sugar for baking.

★ **Marsala or Manzanilla sherry** – for poaching fruits such as figs.

In the fridge

With a few dairy ingredients to enrich and a couple of storecupboard staples, you have a meal in minutes.

★ **Eggs** – the ultimate convenience food. Choose large organic or free-range for scrambled eggs, omelettes and frittatas.

★ **Milk** – choose organic semi-skimmed.

★ **Unsalted butter** – has a superior, more refined flavour than salted and is better for cooking.

★ **Plain Greek yoghurt or bio yoghurt** – yoghurt is very good for adding to curries, or making into dips or quick desserts.

★ **Block of Parmesan cheese** – for grating as you need it on pasta, pizza or salads.

★ **Crème fraîche or double cream** – use to enrich sauces or as an accompaniment for sweet things.

★ **Mascarpone cheese** – this rich cream cheese can make an instant ice cream or tiramisu.

In the freezer

Keep your freezer stocked with foods that can be quickly cooked from frozen – an enormous asset to the time-poor cook.

★ **Fresh chicken and fish stocks** – for gravies, risotto and cooking rice. Avoid stock cubes – instead freeze fresh stock in ice-cube trays.

★ **Good-quality ice cream and sorbet** – store a good-quality vanilla ice cream and a lemon sorbet for an instant pudding.

★ **Mixed summer berries** – great for quick puddings in the winter months.

★ **Mixed seafood and prawns** – can be added to stir-fry dishes without defrosting.

★ **Pastry** – shortcrust, puff and filo are essential for a variety of quick savoury and sweet dishes.

★ **Fish fillets** – such as tuna, cod and haddock.

★ **Frozen vegetables** – if you haven't had a chance to shop for vegetables, make sure you have some in your freezer, such as green beans, petit pois, sweetcorn and spinach.

★ **Frozen chicken breasts** – cut into strips before freezing for quick defrosting.

★ **Ready-to-bake focaccia and ciabatta bread** – a handy standby to accompany meals or for making garlic bread.

no-cook deli suppers

almost-instant dishes

deli pasta

As far as real fast food goes, a bowl of deli pasta ticks all the boxes. Keep your fridge well stocked with a few key deli ingredients and a sustaining and comforting meal is never far from your table (or lap!). My advice is to buy good-quality dried pasta in a variety of shapes and sizes. The only fresh pastas worth buying for everyday eating are the filled varieties, such as ravioli or tortelloni. Always keep a block of fresh Parmesan cheese to hand for grating over your chosen pasta dish.

pappardelle with artichoke hearts and parma ham

This is a quick and simple midweek supper that uses a tub of crème fraîche and some great deli ingredients to create a luxurious pasta dish that even non-cooks can make. If you can't find pappardelle, it will work just as well with tagliatelle.

250 g dried pappardelle (thick ribbons of pasta)

250 ml crème fraîche

1 garlic clove, crushed

1 teaspoon Dijon mustard

140 g roasted and marinated artichoke hearts, drained and cut into small pieces

6 slices (about 40 g) Parma ham, cut into strips

sea salt and freshly ground black pepper

freshly grated Parmesan cheese, to serve

Serves 2

Bring a large pan of salted water to the boil. Add the pasta, cover and bring back to the boil. Remove the lid, stir the pasta and cook according to the packet instructions. The pasta is ready when it is tender but with a central resistance to the bite – *al dente*. When cooked, tip into a colander and drain well, reserving a little of the cooking water.

Add the crème fraîche, garlic and mustard to the pan and bring up to the boil. Add the cooked pasta, artichokes and Parma ham and stir everything together, thinning with a little of the reserved pasta cooking water if necessary. Season to taste with pepper.

Spoon the pasta into warmed serving bowls and sprinkle with Parmesan cheese. Serve immediately.

More quick deli pasta ideas:

★ Spicy tomato fusilli – sunblush tomatoes, crushed garlic, finely chopped red chilli, shredded fresh basil and chilli oil or extra virgin olive oil, tossed through cooked fusilli pasta.

★ Creamy salmon and pea linguine – hot smoked salmon flakes, salmon roe, cooked petit pois, finely chopped fresh dill and crème fraîche, stirred into linguine pasta.

★ Sweet pepper and anchovy penne – deli-style chargrilled red peppers, chopped marinated anchovies, chilli flakes and chopped fresh parsley, added to cooked penne pasta.

★ Creamy bacon and mushroom spaghetti – bacon lardons, chopped marinated wild mushrooms, crushed smoked garlic and crème fraîche, with cooked spaghetti.

★ Cheese and spinach penne – crumbled ricotta, chopped black olives, baby spinach leaves and a drizzle of extra virgin olive oil, tossed through cooked penne pasta.

deli pizza

Freshly made pizza is delicious and surprisingly simple to assemble once you know how to make the most of all the fantastic foods you can buy at your local deli counter.

Keep some ready-made frozen or long-life pizza bases and a few tubs of any basic tomato pasta sauce or a jar of passata (sieved tomatoes) and pesto in your storecupboard (see also pages 136–137). To assemble a super-speedy pizza, first preheat the oven to 200°C (400°F) Gas 6 and put a baking tray in to heat. Next, take a pizza base and spread it generously with a tomato-based pizza topping, pasta sauce, well-seasoned passata or pesto. Select your deli ingredients (see opposite page) and chop or slice them as necessary. Arrange these on the prepared pizza base and season, if necessary, with pepper. When your pizza is assembled, carefully slide it onto the baking tray and place it in the preheated oven. Cook for 10–12 minutes, or until the base is starting to brown at the edges and all the ingredients are warmed through. Drizzle with extra virgin olive oil or a flavoured oil such as chilli, garlic or truffle and grate or shave some fresh Parmesan cheese over the top to finish. Serve with a small bowl of dressed salad leaves – wild rocket or a baby leaf salad are both ideal.

Quick deli pizza ideas – use a 20 to 25 cm (150 g) pizza base per person. Spread the base with your chosen sauce topping and choose a selection of flavours from below:

★ Garlicky mushroom pizza – marinated mushrooms, slices of Taleggio cheese and slivers of smoked garlic.

★ Marinara pizza – antipasti-style marinated seafood (usually a mixture of cooked squid, mussels and prawns), capers and slices of garlic butter. Add a generous handful of wild rocket to the pizza once it's cooked.

★ Mediterraneo pizza – sliced balsamic onions, cubes of feta cheese, pitted black olives, marinated anchovy fillets and a sprinkle of dried mixed herbs or *herbes de Provence*.

★ Italian salami pizza – slices of Napoli or any other Italian-style salami, pitted black olives, sunblush tomatoes, thinly sliced red onions and a few spoonfuls of pesto.

★ Pimiento, tuna and artichoke pizza – chargrilled red peppers, a small tin or jar of tuna steak in olive oil, thinly sliced red onions, marinated artichoke hearts and slices of buffalo mozzarella cheese.

★ Vegetariana pizza – slices of griddled aubergine or courgette, roasted red peppers, ricotta cheese, toasted pine nuts and shredded fresh basil leaves.

★ Spinach and Parma ham pizza – spread baby spinach leaves over a tomato base, then cover with wafer-thin slices of Parma ham and thick slices of mozzarella cheese.

★ Creamy bacon pizza – cooked bacon lardons, a few spoonfuls of mascarpone cheese, thinly sliced red onions and a sprinkle of dried thyme and grated Parmesan cheese.

★ American hot pizza – slices of pepperoni, Jalapeño chillies and thick slices of mozzarella cheese topped with shredded fresh basil leaves.

★ Chicken and blue cheese pizza – shredded roasted chicken breast sprinkled over a base spread with pesto, thinly sliced red onions, cubed Gorgonzola cheese and chopped walnuts.

deli platters

Sharing a deli platter is an effortless and sociable way of eating for busy people. Ask to sample a new cheese or salami before buying at the deli counter and eat French-style by following with a bowl of salad leaves to cleanse the palate. Arrange the foods that you choose on large serving platters and make sure there is plenty of interesting bread on offer. Choose speciality breads such as Irish soda, *pain de Campagne*, baguette, ciabatta, focaccia, bagels, rye, walnut, olive or flatbread crackers and *grissini* (bread sticks).

mixed meats platter

On French and Italian menus you will often find a *charcuterie* or *affettato* platter displaying an array of dried and cured meats. The celeriac remoulade can be made ahead of time and refrigerated.

100 g Milano salami, chorizo sausage or French saucisson
4 slices (about 85 g) Parma or Serrano ham, prosciutto or bresaola
50 g marinated olives (black, green or mixed)
50 g mini gherkins or caper berries, drained and rinsed
100 g wild rocket

For the celeriac remoulade
225 g fresh celeriac, peeled
freshly squeezed juice of ½ a lemon
2 tablespoons good-quality mayonnaise
1 teaspoon Dijon mustard
2 tablespoons chopped fresh tarragon
sea salt and freshly ground black pepper

Serves 2

First make the remoulade. Cut the celeriac into matchstick-sized pieces or, if you find it easier, roughly grate it. Place in a bowl of cold water with the lemon juice to prevent discolouration.

Bring a pan of cold water to the boil, then plunge in the drained celeriac and cook for 1 minute, drain and refresh with cold water, then drain again. Lightly pat dry with a clean tea towel or some kitchen paper. Put the mayonnaise, mustard and tarragon in a large bowl and mix thoroughly. Season to taste. Toss the dried celeriac in the dressing until well coated.

Arrange the cured meats on a large serving platter with the olives, gherkins or caper berries and heap the celeriac remoulade in the centre. Serve the rocket in a separate bowl.

More quick deli platter ideas:

★ Italian-style antipasti platter – arrange chargrilled peppers, roasted and marinated artichoke hearts, sunblush tomatoes and mini mozzarella balls or slices of buffalo mozzarella cheese on a large platter and sprinkle with torn fresh basil. Add caper berries and marinated anchovy fillets. Serve with grilled ciabatta slices rubbed with garlic or some focaccia and a mixed baby leaf salad.

★ Swedish-style smoked fish platter – choose a variety of different smoked fish such as hot smoked salmon, smoked eel, smoked trout, smoked haddock or salmon gravadlax. Accompany with a salad made by tossing peeled and thinly sliced discs of cucumber and shredded fennel with chopped fresh dill and a drop of white wine vinegar. Serve with toasted light rye bread or warmed blinis spread with sour cream.

★ Mixed seafood platter – choose a selection of fresh seafood from the fish counter at your supermarket such as marinated seafood (usually a mixture of cooked squid, mussels and prawns), dressed crab, shell-on tiger prawns, cooked and halved lobster, opened oysters and Green-lipped mussels. Arrange your selection on a platter with some crushed ice. Garnish with fresh lemon and lime wedges. Serve with a bowl of aioli (see pages 97 and 143) and slices of warmed baguette. Don't forget to offer finger bowls and provide plenty of napkins!

★ Cheese ploughman's platter – there are so many fabulous cheeses available, choose a selection of your favourites. A good combination is a ripe *Brie de Meaux* or a creamy vacherin, a tangy Spanish manchego or vintage Cheddar, a blue-veined dolcelatte or Gorgonzola and a fresh goats' cheese. Serve with slices of ripe pear, black grapes and sticks of celery. Add sweet balsamic onions, a good-quality red onion chutney or quince jelly (membrillo) and serve with slices of walnut bread.

This light salad is simplicity itself to prepare. All you need to do is use the best-quality ingredients you can find. Look out at the deli counter for chargrilled red and yellow peppers and roasted or grilled aubergines, but if you can't find them, use ones that are preserved in oil and sold in jars. Do drain them well before using as they can be rather oily.

It makes sense to toast a large batch of pine nuts and keep them in an airtight container so that they are to hand when you want to add them to pasta, pizza and salads.

roasted pepper and aubergine salad

1 tablespoon pine nuts

150 g mixed salad leaves (such as Italian-style)

100 g chargrilled peppers, sliced

100 g roasted aubergines, sliced

50 g feta or firm goats' cheese, crumbled

a handful of fresh basil leaves, shredded

2 tablespoons extra virgin olive oil

freshly ground black pepper

Italian bread, to serve

Serves 2

First toast the pine nuts. Spread out a tablespoonful (or more if toasting a batch) in a thin layer on the base of a large, non-stick frying pan and place over a low heat. Cook over low to medium heat for 2–3 minutes, gently tossing them frequently until they are golden brown. Remove from the heat and set aside until needed.

Put the salad leaves, peppers, aubergines, toasted pine nuts, cheese and shredded basil in a large bowl. Add the olive oil, season well with pepper and toss until evenly coated with the seasoned oil.

Arrange the prepared salad on serving plates and serve immediately with a basket of good Italian bread, such as ciabatta or Pugliese.

Variation: Add a few slices of Parma ham and some pitted black olives to the salad.

If you've had a busy day and are home too late for a heavy meal, then this snack supper is ideal. Enjoy it with a glass of chilled white wine – French Vouvray is perfect.

Gravadlax is a Swedish speciality – very fresh, raw salmon fillet is cured with dill, sugar, salt and coarse peppercorns. It is widely available in supermarkets and often packed with a sachet of dill-flavoured mustard sauce, which can be rather overpowering. I like to mix a tablespoon of sauce with two tablespoons of crème fraîche.

gravadlax and pickled cucumber open sandwich

200 g cucumber

1 teaspoon white wine vinegar

½ teaspoon chopped fresh dill

freshly ground black pepper (or mixed peppercorns)

2 slices light rye or Irish soda bread

2 tablespoons crème fraîche

100 g gravadlax

Serves 2

Peel the cucumber and halve it lengthways. Scoop out the seeds using a teaspoon and cut it into wafer-thin, crescent-shaped slices. Pat these dry with kitchen paper and put them in a large bowl.

Put the vinegar and chopped dill in a small bowl, season with a little freshly ground black pepper (or mixed peppercorns) and use a fork to combine. Pour the dressing over the cucumber and toss to coat.

Lightly toast the rye or soda bread and, while it's still warm, spread generously with crème fraîche. Top with the marinated cucumber salad and slices of gravadlax. Serve immediately with the remaining crème fraîche separately.

Strictly speaking this isn't a 'no-cook' recipe as the potatoes need to be boiled. But, if you are really short of time, buy a tub of good-quality ready-made potato salad and mix it with half the amount of the dill dressing.

For a variation, I sometimes use Swedish pickled herrings instead of the smoked trout – they give the dish even more Swedish style.

After opening a bottle of beer for the dressing, it would seem wasteful not to enjoy a glass of it with the salad!

smoked trout, warm new potato and beetroot salad

125 g small new potatoes, halved if large

sea salt and freshly ground black pepper

For the dill dressing

1 teaspoon wholegrain mustard

1 tablespoon beer or lager

1 teaspoon caster sugar

2 tablespoons extra virgin olive oil

2 tablespoons chopped fresh dill, plus extra sprigs to garnish

125 g smoked trout fillets, skinned and flaked

2 cooked fresh beetroot (not pickled), sliced into wedges

1 head of chicory, thickly sliced

Irish soda bread or similar, to serve

Serves 2

Put the potatoes in a large pan, add sufficient cold water to cover, add a little salt and bring to the boil. Cook for 10–15 minutes until just tender.

Meanwhile, make the dressing. Put the mustard, beer or lager, sugar, olive oil and chopped dill in a small bowl and use a small whisk or fork to combine.

Drain the potatoes and, when cool enough to handle, slice thickly and put in a bowl with half of the dressing. Toss to coat.

Arrange the trout fillet flakes, slices of warm dressed potato, beetroot wedges and chicory on serving plates and garnish with the sprigs of dill. Drizzle the remaining dressing over the top and serve immediately, with slices of warm Irish soda bread or similar.

This makes a lovely change from prawn cocktail! Buy the juiciest-looking cooked prawns you can find and leave them in the marinade for as long as possible. I use pink grapefruit as it looks prettier and tastes sweeter than the white variety.

chilli tiger prawn salad

For the prawns

1 garlic clove, crushed

freshly squeezed juice of 1 lime

2 tablespoons sweet chilli sauce

200 g cooked tiger prawns, peeled but tails left intact

1 pink grapefruit

2 tablespoons extra virgin olive oil

100 g cherry tomatoes, halved

1 small, ripe avocado, peeled, stoned and diced

½ red onion, thinly sliced

a handful of fresh coriander leaves

garlic bread or similar, to serve

Serves 2

First prepare the prawns. Put the garlic, lime juice and sweet chilli sauce in a shallow, non-metallic container and whisk with a fork to combine. Add the prawns, stir to coat with the mixture, cover and set aside in a cool place to marinate whilst you prepare the rest of the salad.

Cut away the peel and pith from the grapefruit with a serrated knife. Hold the grapefruit in the palm of your hand and cut away each segment, working over a large bowl to catch the juices.

Add the olive oil to the grapefruit juice and whisk with a fork to combine. Add the grapefruit segments, cherry tomatoes, avocado, red onion and coriander to the bowl and toss to combine.

Divide the prepared salad between serving plates, or glasses for a cocktail effect. Remove the prawns from their marinade (using tongs or a slotted spoon) and arrange them on top. Drizzle the remaining marinade over the salad. Serve immediately with slices of warm garlic bread or similar.

This winning combination of smoked chicken, mango, fresh coriander and lime makes this a summery salad with a bit of zing! As there is no need to cook the chicken, all that's left to do is make the dressing and assemble the salad.

This recipe would also work well if you have a few friends coming over. Use a whole smoked chicken (about 1.2 kg in size), and double up the remaining ingredients. If you can't find smoked chicken, use a mixture of cooked chicken and smoked ham instead.

smoked chicken, mango and lime salad

1 large, ripe mango

juice and finely grated zest of 1 lime

3 tablespoons light olive oil

1 tablespoon finely chopped fresh coriander, plus extra sprigs to garnish

2 boneless smoked chicken breasts (about 325 g total weight)

100 g cos lettuce leaves

1 spring onion, thinly sliced

sea salt and freshly ground black pepper

extra virgin olive oil, to serve

Serves 2

Remove the skin and stone of the mango, then chop the flesh. Put in a food processor or blender with the lime juice, blitz until smooth, then gradually add the olive oil in a thin stream with the motor running until the mixture begins to thicken. Pour the dressing into a large bowl and stir in the chopped coriander and lime zest.

Slice the chicken into bite-sized pieces and put it in the bowl with the dressing. Toss the chicken until coated in the dressing. Arrange the lettuce on serving plates, drizzle with a little extra virgin olive oil and season with salt and pepper.

Spoon the chicken with the mango dressing over the leaves and scatter with spring onion and coriander sprigs to finish. Serve immediately.

Picking up a hot, rotisserie-cooked chicken from the supermarket is the perfect answer for commuters and busy parents. The warm chicken flesh slightly softens the cheese making the salad taste even more delectable, so do try and get your chicken home quickly and use it while it's still warm!

This is a good salad to serve at Christmas as you can use Stilton cheese and leftover turkey instead of chicken.

roast chicken, watercress and blue cheese salad

small (about 1.3 kg) rotisserie-cooked chicken, preferably still warm

100 g watercress

1 cos lettuce, chopped

50 g walnuts pieces

1 red dessert apple, quartered, cored and thinly sliced

sea salt and freshly ground black pepper

freshly squeezed juice of ½ lemon

1 tablespoon extra virgin olive oil

50 g Roquefort, Gorgonzola or Stilton, cut into cubes

baguette, to serve

Serves 2

Remove the flesh from the roast chicken carcass, including the wings and the legs. Cut it into bite-sized pieces.

Put the chicken pieces in a bowl with the watercress, lettuce, walnut pieces and apple slices. Season well and add the lemon juice and olive oil. Toss well so that the salad is evenly coated with the dressing.

Divide the dressed salad between serving plates and arrange the cheese cubes amongst the leaves. Serve immediately with generous slices of warm baguette.

simple suppers
fuss-free recipes for two

Couscous is an excellent storecupboard staple for the busy cook as it doesn't need cooking – it is simply soaked in water or stock and fluffed up with a fork. It is classically served with a rich North African stew prepared in a tagine as it acts like an absorbent sponge and mops up the sauce. This roasted vegetable couscous is spicy and satisfying. If time is very short, look out for pre-packed, peeled and chopped vegetables from supermarkets as using these will greatly reduce the preparation time.

moroccan-style roasted vegetable couscous

175 g red onions

175 g sweet potato

175 g red peppers

175 g leeks

2 garlic cloves, halved

2 tablespoons olive oil

½ teaspoon dried chilli flakes

150 g couscous

300 ml hot vegetable stock or water

a handful of fresh mint sprigs

freshly squeezed lemon juice, to taste

sea salt and freshly ground black pepper

a non-stick baking tray or small roasting tin

Serves 2

Preheat the oven to 200°C (400°F) Gas 6.

Remove the thin skin from the onions and slice them into thin wedges. Peel the sweet potato and cut into chunks. Core and deseed the peppers, then chop. Trim the leeks, then split them and wash well. Dry with kitchen paper and cut into large chunks.

Put the prepared vegetables and garlic on a non-stick baking tray or in a small roasting tin. Pour the olive oil over the top, add the chilli flakes and use your hands to toss the vegetables until they are coated with the oil mixture. Place the tray or tin in the preheated oven and cook for about 20–25 minutes, or until golden and tender.

Meanwhile, put the couscous in a large bowl and pour over the hot vegetable stock or water. Cover and set aside until the couscous swells and absorbs all the liquid, about 10 minutes.

Use a fork to fluff up the couscous, then add the roasted vegetables and mint sprigs. Add a little lemon juice and season to taste. Serve immediately whilst still warm.

Variation: Add 50 g crumbled or diced feta cheese to the couscous.

You can save time and washing up here by cooking the broccoli in the same pan as the pasta. If it's in season, use purple sprouting broccoli. Trim the fiborous ends, then slice into 1-cm lengths, dividing the florets into bite-sized pieces.

The anchovy is already very salty, so it's best to taste a forkful before adding any more salt.

tagliatelle with broccoli, anchovy, parmesan and crème fraîche

175 g dried tagliatelle

300 g broccoli florets

1 tablespoon olive oil

2 garlic cloves, crushed

½ teaspoon dried chilli flakes

3 anchovy fillets, roughly chopped

100 g crème fraîche

sea salt and freshly ground black pepper

freshly grated Parmesan cheese, to serve

Serves 2

Bring a large pan of salted water to the boil. Add the pasta, cover with a lid and bring back to the boil. Remove the lid, stir the pasta and cook according to the packet instructions. Add the broccoli to the pasta 3–4 minutes before the end of cooking. Drain the pasta and the broccoli well and reserve a little of the cooking water.

Wipe out the pan and add the olive oil. Cook the garlic, chilli flakes and anchovies over low heat for about 2 minutes. Add the crème fraîche, season with a little pepper and bring to the boil. Return the cooked broccoli and pasta to the pan, adding a little of the reserved pasta cooking water if necessary to thin the sauce down. Season to taste with black pepper.

Divide the pasta between serving bowls and serve immediately, sprinkled with Parmesan cheese.

Halloumi is a firm Greek cheese that is delicious eaten when hot and melting. It has a reasonably long shelf-life before it is opened, which means you can keep a pack tucked away in the fridge. Harissa is a fiery chilli paste used in North African cooking – add more if you like your food spicy.

1 tablespoon olive oil

1 onion, finely chopped

1 garlic clove, crushed

1 tablespoon harissa paste (see note below)

400-g tin chickpeas, drained

400-g tin chopped tomatoes (flavoured with garlic or mixed herbs, if available)

125 g halloumi cheese, cut into cubes

100 g baby spinach leaves

sea salt and freshly ground black pepper

freshly squeezed juice of ½ lemon

freshly grated Parmesan cheese and crisp green salad, to serve

Serves 2

harissa-spiced chickpeas
with halloumi and spinach

Pour the oil into a large pan and gently sauté the onion and garlic until softened. Add the harissa paste, chickpeas and chopped tomatoes. Bring to the boil and let simmer for about 5 minutes.

Add the halloumi cheese and spinach, cover and cook over a low heat for a further 5 minutes. Season to taste and stir in the lemon juice. Spoon onto serving plates and sprinkle with the Parmesan cheese. Serve immediately with a crisp green side salad.

Variation: Substitute a 400-g tin of any beans (such as borlotti, kidney or cannellini) for the chickpeas.

Note: If you don't have harissa paste, you can make your own by mixing together ½ teaspoon cayenne pepper, 1 tablespoon ground cumin, 1 tablespoon tomato purée and the freshly squeezed juice of 1 lime.

Risotto is a relatively simple dish to make. You have to watch the rice like a hawk and a good deal of stirring is required, but you can multi-task and rustle up a salad while it's cooking! Remember to keep the stock nice and hot and the heat constant. Roasting the squash first brings out its sweetness and the pumpkin seeds add a spicy crunch.

roasted butternut squash risotto

500 g butternut squash, peeled, deseeded and diced

3 tablespoons olive oil

1½ teaspoons dried chilli flakes

sea salt and freshly ground black pepper

25 g pumpkin seeds

850 ml vegetable stock

1 small onion, finely chopped

150 g Arborio rice

100 ml white wine

50 g Parmesan cheese, finely grated

crème fraîche, to serve

a small roasting tin

Serves 2

Preheat the oven to 230°C (450°F) Gas 8.

Put the butternut squash in a small roasting tin with 1 tablespoon of the olive oil, ½ teaspoon of the chilli flakes and season well. Toss the squash in the seasoned oil until it is evenly coated. Put in the preheated oven and cook for about 20 minutes, or until soft and golden. (Use a large spoon to turn the squash at regular intervals while it is cooking.)

Heat 1 tablespoon of the remaining olive oil in a small frying pan and toast the pumpkin seeds with the remaining chilli flakes for about 1–2 minutes until lightly browned. Set aside until needed.

Whilst the squash is cooking in the oven, make the risotto. Pour the vegetable stock into a large pan and heat to a simmer. Pour the remaining oil into a high-sided pan and gently sauté the onion over medium heat for about 1 minute, or until softened. Add the rice, stir for 2–3 minutes, then add the wine and let simmer until reduced by half. Add another ladleful of hot stock. Let the risotto continue to simmer gently, adding another ladleful or two of stock each time the liquid has been absorbed into the rice. Stir, almost continuously, until the rice has absorbed all the stock.

Once the rice is cooked and tender, stir in the roasted butternut squash and the Parmesan cheese and season to taste. Serve immediately, topped with a little crème fraîche and sprinkled with the toasted pumpkin seeds.

Keeping a bag of mixed seafood in the freezer is a great standby for a fast supper. It can be added frozen to rice dishes, pasta or soup – just make sure they are cooked for an extra few minutes and are piping hot.

stir-fried seafood
with vegetables and a balsamic dressing

2 tablespoons olive oil

1 red pepper, cored, deseeded and cut into thin strips

2 leeks, trimmed and cut into strips

1 large onion, cut into thick wedges

150 g cherry tomatoes, halved

2 garlic cloves, finely sliced

1 teaspoon dried chilli flakes

300 g frozen mixed seafood, such as prawns, mussels, scallops and squid rings, either defrosted or frozen

a few fresh coriander sprigs, to garnish

2 teaspoons balsamic vinegar

a large frying pan or wok

Serves 2

Heat 1 tablespoon of the oil in a large frying pan or wok. Add the peppers, leeks and onion and stir-fry over high heat until lightly brown. Add the cherry tomatoes and cook for a further 2 minutes. Remove the vegetables from the pan and set aside in a warm place until needed.

Heat the remaining oil in the same frying pan or wok. Add the garlic, chilli flakes and mixed seafood and stir-fry over high heat. Cook for 3–4 minutes, stirring occasionally (increase the cooking time to 7–8 minutes if the seafood is frozen).

Mix the warm vegetables with the seafood and add the balsamic vinegar and coriander at the last moment. Serve immediately.

If you have ever tasted the classic French fish soup *bouillabaisse* and enjoyed the flavour, then this is a good cheat's version. The combination of saffron, orange and fennel gives the stew its distinctive flavour. If you can't find Noilly Prat, use dry Martini or a dry white wine in its place.

If you have time to make the base of the stew the day before you plan to eat it, the flavours will develop even further – simply cook the fish at the last moment.

mediterranean chunky fish stew with cheese toasts

1 small onion, finely chopped

2 garlic cloves, 1 crushed; 1 peeled and halved

a pinch of dried thyme

125 g fennel, hard core removed and finely chopped

1 tablespoon olive oil

50 ml Noilly Prat, dry Martini or dry white wine

400 g passata (sieved tomatoes)

1 pinch of saffron threads

freshly squeezed juice and grated zest of 1 orange

200 g skinless cod fillet, cut into large chunks

sea salt and freshly ground black pepper (optional)

4 thin slices of baguette

50 g Emmental or Gruyère cheese, grated

Serves 2

In a large pan, gently sauté the chopped onion, crushed garlic, thyme and fennel in the olive oil for about 6–8 minutes or until soft. Add the Noilly Prat, dry Martini or dry white wine and let bubble, uncovered, until the liquid has almost reduced to nothing.

Add the passata, saffron, orange juice and zest and 200 ml cold water. Raise the heat and cook for 10 minutes. Add the cod fillet and cook gently for a further 2 minutes, then taste and season if necessary.

Meanwhile, preheat the grill to high. Toast the baguette slices on each side under the grill until lightly golden. Rub the halved garlic over each slice and sprinkle with the grated cheese.

Ladle the stew into warmed deep serving bowls and balance the cheese-topped toasts on top. Serve immediately.

Rather than brown the chicken breast in a pan, you simply season it and let the oven do all the work. There is a lot of garlic in this dish, but the flavour becomes much more subtle once the garlic is blanched.

roast chicken with garlic, apple and cider

4 garlic cloves, peeled but left whole

2 boneless chicken breasts with skin (each weighing about 130 g), lightly beaten if thick

sea salt and freshly ground black pepper

2 tablespoons olive oil

100 ml dry cider

1 red dessert apple, peeled, quartered, cored and diced

2 tablespoons Dijon mustard

100 ml crème fraîche

a handful of chopped fresh parsley

purple sprouting broccoli spears and new potatoes, to serve

a baking tray

Serves 2

Preheat the oven to 200°C (400°F) Gas 6.

Bring a small pan of water to the boil and cook the garlic cloves for 2–3 minutes, or until tender. Drain and set aside until needed.

Season the chicken breasts and drizzle with the olive oil. Put them on a baking tray and place on the top shelf of the preheated oven to cook for about 25 minutes, or until the chicken is cooked through and the skin is golden.

Meanwhile, put the garlic, cider, chopped apple and mustard in a large frying pan. Cook gently over a low heat for about 10 minutes.

When the chicken is cooked, remove it from the oven and transfer to the pan. Add the crème fraîche to the pan and simmer for 5 minutes. Use the back of a fork to squash the garlic down into the sauce, taking care not to squash the apples too. Season to taste. Stir in the parsley and serve immediately, with broccoli spears and new potatoes.

Variations: This classic French sauce also works well with oven-roasted or grilled pork chops. Instead of new potatoes, serve pasta as an accompaniment. Pour a little sauce over cooked tagliatelle and toss until the pasta is evenly coated. Serve this with the chicken or pork instead of new potatoes.

You can add your choice of vegetables to this basic curry recipe, such as sliced mushrooms, trimmed French beans, fresh spinach, bamboo shoots or sticks of courgette and carrot – it's perfect for using up odds and ends. Jasmine or fragrant rice is a delicately scented white rice native to Thailand. If you are very short on time, use one of the excellent brands that is microwavable in the packet.

quick thai chicken curry

400-ml tin coconut milk

50 g green Thai curry paste

1 tablespoon sunflower oil

1 chicken breast (weighing about 400 g), cut into bite-sized pieces

½ teaspoon kaffir lime leaf purée

1 teaspoon Thai fish sauce

100 g mixed fresh vegetables of your choice (see above)

a handful of fresh basil leaves

For the jasmine rice

200 g Thai jasmine or fragrant rice

25 g unsalted butter

a pinch of sea salt

a large frying pan or wok

Serves 2

To make the jasmine rice, put the rice in a large pan that has a tight-fitting lid. Add 375 ml cold water, the butter and salt. Bring it to the boil, and turn down the heat to a simmer. Cook and cook over low heat, covered, for 20 minutes or until the rice has absorbed all the liquid (add a little more water if the rice is not yet tender).

Meanwhile, pour the coconut milk into a saucepan and gently bring it to near boiling. Remove the saucepan from the heat and stir in the Thai curry paste. Put to one side.

Pour the oil into a large frying pan or wok and stir-fry the chicken pieces over high heat until golden, about 2 minutes.

Pour the warm, spiced coconut milk over the fried chicken pieces and add the kaffir lime leaf purée and fish sauce. Add any vegetables you are using at this stage. Stir and simmer gently for about 12 minutes, or until everything is cooked through.

Remove the cooked rice from the heat and let sit for 5 minutes. Fluff it up with a fork just before serving. Scatter the basil over the curry and serve it with a small bowl of rice on the side.

The juiciness of the grilled tomatoes gives the meat a natural sauce and the creamy soft polenta makes a great alternative to mashed potatoes. If you use a fresh chicken stock, it will make all the difference to the flavour of the instant polenta – look out for these above the poultry counter in your supermarket. If you have an aversion to goats' cheese, simply omit it from the polenta. The trick to tender steaks is to take the meat out of the fridge 15 minutes before you intend to cook it, then make sure you cook the meat fast over a scorchingly high heat.

beef steak with goats' cheese polenta and grilled tomatoes

300 ml chicken stock

75 g instant polenta

25 g unsalted butter

75 g firm goats' cheese, crumbled

sea salt and freshly ground black pepper

a crisp green salad, to serve

200 g plum or beefsteak tomatoes

1 tablespoon extra virgin olive oil

a few drops of balsamic vinegar

2 sirloin, rump or fillet steaks (each weighing about 175 g)

crisp green salad, to serve

a heavy-based stove-top grill pan or griddle

Serves 2

Pour the chicken stock into a large pan and bring it to the boil. Remove from the heat and slowly add the polenta, pouring from a jug and whisking until all of it has been added. Return the pan to the heat and cook until the polenta thickens and falls away from the side of the pan. Beat in the butter and goats' cheese and season to taste with salt and pepper.

Cut the tomatoes in half lengthways and sprinkle with salt and pepper. Heat the oil in a heavy-based stove-top grill pan and cook for 2 minutes on one side before turning them over and cooking briefly on the other side. Drizzle with the balsamic vinegar. Remove from the pan and set aside in a warm place.

Season the steaks on both sides. Place a heavy-based stove-top grill pan or griddle over high heat until very hot indeed. Quickly drop each steak directly in the pan. Sear them quickly on both sides. Turn the heat down and cook them for 2–3 minutes on each side (for medium rare – see guide on page 58).

Lift the steaks onto warmed serving plates and add a few generous spoonfuls of the polenta and the grilled tomatoes. Serve with a crisp green side salad.

This is a cheat's version of a Spanish peasant stew called a *fabada* – beans, sausage and a rich tomato and red wine sauce make a welcoming supper on a cold winter's evening. If you can't get hold of chorizo, any spicy sausage will do. It is especially good with a glass of Spanish Rioja.

spanish sausage and butter bean tagine

1 tablespoon olive oil

1 onion, finely chopped

2 garlic cloves, crushed

75 g chorizo sausage, skin removed and cut into 1-cm slices

100 ml red wine

400-g tin chopped tomatoes

1 red onion, cut into thin petals

400-g tin butter beans, drained

1 teaspoon dried mixed herbs

a few fresh rosemary or thyme sprigs

sea salt and freshly ground black pepper

2 tablespoons of finely, freshly grated Parmesan cheese

warm crusty bread, to serve

Serves 2

Heat the oil in a large, high-sided frying pan. Add the chopped onion and garlic and cook for a few minutes over medium heat. Add the chorizo sausage and cook for a further 2–3 minutes.

Add the red wine and bring to the boil. Allow to bubble until the mixture is reduced by half. Add the tomatoes, red onion petals, butter beans, 100 ml water and the dried mixed herbs and rosemary or thyme sprigs. Simmer, uncovered for about 10 minutes.

Season to taste with salt and pepper and spoon into warmed serving bowls. Sprinkle with the Parmesan cheese and serve immediately with chunks of warm crusty bread to mop up the juices.

A frittata is Italy's version of an open omelette and it wins hands down as one of the most convenient ways to use up leftover bits and bobs in the fridge. This one is packed with tasty chargrilled peppers and pepperoni, and must be served immediately, otherwise it goes on cooking and loses its soft creaminess. It can also be left to cool, cut into wedges and enjoyed as part of a lunch-on-the-go the following day.

pepperoni, red pepper and croûton frittata

4 eggs, lightly beaten

sea salt and freshly ground black pepper

25 g Gruyère cheese, grated

1 spring onion, thinly sliced

25 g unsalted butter

50 g firm white bread, torn into small pieces

1 garlic clove, crushed

25 g chargrilled red peppers, cut into strips

25 g pepperoni, sliced

a crisp green salad or a tomato and basil salad, to serve

a medium-sized, ovenproof frying pan

Serves 2

Break the eggs into a bowl and beat well using a fork. Season well with salt and pepper and add half the cheese and spring onion. Mix well.

Melt half the butter in a medium-sized, ovenproof frying pan. Add the bread pieces and toss them for 2–3 minutes over high heat until golden brown and crispy. Remove from the heat and set aside.

Preheat the grill to medium. Add the remaining butter and the garlic to the pan, and when the butter starts to froth, add the beaten eggs. Turn the heat down and leave the eggs to cook gently for a few minutes. Arrange the pepperoni and chargrilled peppers on the top and sprinkle with the remaining cheese and reserved croutons.

Put the frying pan under the preheated grill and cook for a further 2–3 minutes until the frittatta is puffed and just set but still wobbly. Remove from the grill and serve immediately with a crisp green salad or a tomato and basil salad.

Variation: Also delicious made with any combination of the following: crumbled firm goats' cheese, sliced mushrooms, baby spinach leaves, courgettes or sliced cooked potatoes.

These delicious little pancake rolls could not be easier to make. Chinese pancakes are available in specialist Asian shops and most supermarkets, but if you can't find them use ready-made small flour tortillas or 'batter' pancakes.

chinese duck pancakes

2 duck breasts with skin (each weighing about 150g)

2 teaspoons sea salt flakes

1 teaspoon Chinese five-spice powder

6–8 Chinese pancakes or small flour tortillas or 4 ready-made 'batter' pancakes

1 spring onion, thinly sliced

½ cucumber, deseeded and thinly sliced

a handful of fresh coriander sprigs, finely chopped

1 small red chilli, finely chopped

4 tablespoons hoisin or plum sauce

an ovenproof frying pan

Serves 2

Preheat the oven to 200°C (400°F) Gas 6.

Rub the skin of the duck breasts with the salt and Chinese five-spice powder. Heat an ovenproof frying pan or skillet, and cook the breasts skin-side down until golden. Place the frying pan in the oven and continue to cook the breasts for a further 10–15 minutes or until tender but still pink in the centre.

To serve, either steam the pancakes or place in a microwave for a few minutes until piping hot (check the packet instructions).

Slice the duck breasts and finely shred the meat, then place it on a warmed serving plate. Arrange the spring onion, cucumber, coriander sprigs, chilli and hoisin or plum sauce in separate piles on a wooden board and/or in small bowls.

To serve, dig in and help yourselves. Take a warm Chinese pancake or small tortilla and spread it with a teaspoonful of sauce. Place some duck, spring onion, cucumber, coriander and chilli in the centre, roll up and eat with your fingers.

This simple recipe is bursting with Greek flavours. If you marinate any meat in yoghurt it becomes incredibly tender, so the longer you can leave it in before cooking the better.

minted lamb pitas with red onion and tomato salad

325 g lamb escalopes or steaks, trimmed of fat

200 g plum tomatoes, chopped

1 small red onion, thinly sliced into discs

2 tablespoons extra virgin olive oil

1 teaspoon balsamic vinegar

2 wholemeal pita breads

lemon wedges, to serve

For the marinade

3 tablespoons Greek yoghurt

1 garlic clove, crushed

2 tablespoons finely chopped fresh mint, plus extra leaves for the salad

a squeeze of fresh lemon juice, plus extra for the lamb

½ teaspoon ground cumin

sea salt and freshly ground black pepper

a heavy-based stove-top grill pan or griddle

Serves 2

First make the marinade. Mix together the yoghurt, garlic, chopped mint, lemon juice, cumin and salt and pepper to taste in a bowl. Put the steaks on a plate and smother each piece with the yoghurt marinade. Cover and leave in a cool place to marinate for a few minutes.

While the lamb is marinating, mix together the tomatoes, red onion, mint sprigs, 1 tablespoon of the olive oil, balsamic vinegar and salt and pepper to taste.

Remove the lamb from the yoghurt marinade. Brush a heavy-based stove-top grill pan or griddle with the remaining oil and heat until smoking. Cook the lamb for about 3 minutes on each side.

Meanwhile, briefly run the pita breads under running water and put in a toaster or under a preheated high grill for a few minutes. They should puff up but not become brown and crisp. Sprinkle the cooked lamb with a squeeze of lemon juice and slice thickly. Split the pita breads open and fill with the tomato salad and slices of lamb.

Variation: The yoghurt marinade works well with chicken fillets that have been lightly beaten flat before marinating.

Look out for a dark piece of steak with a little bit of creamy fat running through it – bright red meat is likely to be tough. Sichuan peppercorns are often used in Chinese cooking to add a woody aroma and peppery flavour. If you can't find them, you can use Chinese five-spice powder instead.

If you don't have time to make a flavoured butter, look out for the ready-made garlic and herb ones.

peppered steak sandwich
with local market salad

25 g flavoured butter (see pages 138–139)

2 sirloin or fillet steaks (each weighing about 150 g)

1 tablespoon olive oil, plus extra for oiling

1 tablespoon Sichuan peppercorns, crushed

1 teaspoon sea salt flakes

1 ripe avocado, peeled, stoned and chopped

150 g cherry tomatoes, halved

120 g fennel, hard core removed and thinly finely

85-g bag watercress

75-g bag curly endive salad

1 baguette, halved horizontally, to serve

For the herb vinaigrette

1 tablespoon white wine or tarragon vinegar

1 tablespoon Dijon mustard

4 tablespoons extra virgin olive oil

1 teaspoon caster sugar

1 tablespoon chopped fresh tarragon

a heavy-based stove-top grill pan or griddle

Serves 2

First make the flavoured butter of your choice and chill it in the fridge until needed. Lightly score each side of the steaks and rub with the olive oil. Sprinkle the crushed Sichuan peppercorns and salt onto a plate and roll the steaks in the seasoning (if time allows, cover and leave for a while before cooking). Lightly oil a heavy-based stove-top grill pan or griddle and heat until very hot indeed. Quickly drop each steak directly in the pan. Sear quickly on both sides. Turn the heat down and cook them for about 2–3 minutes on each side, depending on how you like your steak cooked (see below). Cover with foil, and leave to rest for about 5 minutes.

Meanwhile, put the avocado in a large bowl. Add the cherry tomatoes, fennel, watercress and curly endive salad. Put all the ingredients for the vinaigrette in a screw-top jar and shake vigorously until evenly combined.

Toss the salad with a little of the herb vinaigrette (any leftover vinaigrette can be stored in the fridge for up to 1 week). Divide the salad between 2 halves of the baguette. Place slices of steak in each and serve immediately.

Cooking steak: Rare, medium or well done? A great tip for testing steaks doneness is to use your face as a guide. Lightly press your (clean) finger onto the surface of the meat; if it feels like your cheek it's rare, if it feels like your nose it's medium and if it feels like your forehead it's well done.

light bites

soups and salads for two

Once everything is peeled and chopped, this country-style chunky soup is surprisingly simple to make. The vegetables are roasted in the oven, which makes their flavour sweet but intense, so all you need to do is throw them in a blender or food processor for an instant and nutritious supper. If you prefer a smoother texture, just push it through a sieve once cooked.

roasted vegetable soup

700 g ripe plum tomatoes, halved

175 g red onions, finely chopped

150 g carrots, peeled and finely chopped

1 small red chilli, left whole

2 garlic cloves, peeled but left whole

a few fresh thyme or rosemary sprigs

2 tablespoons olive oil

350 ml passata (sieved tomatoes)

½ teaspoon sugar

a squeeze of fresh lime juice

sea salt and freshly ground black pepper

a handful of fresh coriander, roughly chopped

a drizzle of extra virgin olive oil

and warm crusty bread, to serve

a roasting tin

Serves 2

Preheat the oven to 200°C (400°F) Gas 6.

Put the plum tomatoes, onions and carrots in a roasting tin. Add the chilli, garlic, thyme or rosemary sprigs and olive oil and toss until the vegetables are well coated. Place in the preheated oven and roast for about 25 minutes, turning the vegetables occasionally using a large spoon.

Remove from the oven and discard the chilli. Blend the roasted vegetables, garlic and herbs with the passata in a blender or food processor, using a hand-held blender. Add the sugar, lime juice and 150 ml cold water, and season well with salt and pepper.

Pour the mixture into a large pan and gently heat through. Add the chopped coriander just before serving. Ladle into warmed serving bowls and drizzle with a little extra virgin olive oil. Serve immediately with warm crusty bread.

Root vegetable crisps make a delicious crunchy topping for this comforting soup, which also works well with pumpkin.

spiced butternut squash and coconut soup

25 g unsalted butter

1 large white onion, roughly chopped

185 g carrots, peeled and roughly chopped

500 g butternut squash, peeled, deseeded and cubed

½ teaspoon ground cumin

1 teaspoon Madras curry powder

400 ml vegetable stock

1 tablespoon muscovado sugar

170 ml tinned coconut milk, plus extra to garnish

freshly squeezed juice of ½ lime

sea salt and freshly ground black pepper

a handful of fresh coriander, chopped

Serves 2–4

Melt the butter in a large saucepan over low heat. Add the onion, carrot and squash and gently sauté for 5–8 minutes, stirring occasionally, until the vegetables begin to soften. Add the cumin and curry powder and stir over medium heat for 1 minute until the vegetables are well coated with the spices.

Stir in the stock, sugar and coconut milk and let simmer for about 20 minutes, or until the vegetables are cooked through and soft.

Blend the soup until smooth, either in a blender or food processor, or using a hand-held blender. Taste and season with salt and pepper, then add the lime juice. Stir in the chopped coriander. Pour the soup into warmed bowls and swirl some extra coconut milk over the top. Serve immediately.

These spicy crisps make the perfect accompaniment for light dishes such as Chilli Scallops (page 93).

spiced sweet potato chips

350 g sweet potatoes, peeled and sliced into thin discs

2 tablespoons soy sauce

2 tablespoons olive oil

a handful of fresh coriander, chopped

crème fraîche, to serve

a non-stick roasting tin

Serves 4

Preheat the oven to 220°C (425°F) Gas 7.

Mix together the oil and soy sauce. Place the sweet potato discs in a non-stick roasting tin in an even, single layer. Pour the oil mixture over the sweet potato and toss the discs until they are coated.

Bake in the preheated oven for 20 minutes or until golden and cooked through. Serve immediately with crème fraîche for dipping.

This is a wonderful meal-in-a-bowl that takes only minutes to put together. It is quite spicy, so reduce the quantity of chilli if you prefer. Tom yum paste is a treasure to have in your storecupboard if you have a fondness for Thai food. Use it for stir-fries or Thai curries.

tom yum prawn noodle soup

100 g uncooked large or king prawns, shells on

2 tablespoons tom yum paste

1 red chilli, seeded and finely chopped

1 red pepper, deseeded and thinly sliced

100 g brown cap mushrooms, sliced

100 g leeks, trimmed and finely diced

100 g rice noodles

a few fresh coriander sprigs, to garnish

freshly squeezed juice of 1 lime

Serves 2–4

Peel the prawns and use a very sharp knife to cut each one along the back so that it opens out like a butterfly (leaving each prawn joined along the base and at the tail). Remove the black vein.

Bring 570 ml water to the boil in a large pan . Stir in the tom yum paste until dissolved. Add the chilli, red pepper, mushrooms and leeks and let the mixture simmer for 5 minutes.

Meanwhile, put the noodles in a large heatproof bowl, cover with boiling water and leave to sit for 3–5 minutes until just tender before draining in a colander and spooning into deep serving bowls.

Add the prawns to the tom yum mixture and simmer for a further 2–3 minutes. Pour the tum yum soup over the noodles. Squeeze a little lime juice over each bowl and garnish with a coriander sprig. Serve immediately.

This oriental rice soup can be enjoyed as a snack at any time, but it's sustaining enough to make a light meal, and it's great if you have a cold. For the best flavour, look out for fresh chicken stock sold in tubs – or, better still, when you cook a chicken, make a batch of stock for the freezer.

chicken, lemongrass, ginger and rice soup

50 g Basmati rice

500 ml chicken stock

1½ tablespoons light soy sauce

½ teaspoon dried chilli flakes

½ lemongrass stalk, outer leaves removed, finely chopped

½-cm piece of ginger root, peeled and finely chopped

2 garlic cloves, thinly sliced

3 chicken breasts (each about 150 g), cut into small pieces

1 red pepper, cored, deseeded and thinly sliced

3 spring onions, finely chopped

50 g Chinese cabbage, finely shredded (optional)

a squeeze of fresh lime juice

freshly ground black pepper

fresh coriander leaves, to garnish

Serves 2–4

Cook the rice according to the packet instructions. Drain, rinse, drain again and set aside until needed.

Heat the stock to boiling point in a large pan. Add the soy sauce, chilli flakes, lemongrass, ginger and garlic, and cook over high heat for 5 minutes.

Add the chicken pieces and red pepper and let the mixture gently bubble for about 3 minutes, or until the chicken is tender.

Add the cooked rice and cook for a further 1 minute. Finally, stir in the spring onions and cabbage (if using). Ladle into warmed bowls. Squeeze a little lime juice over each, season with pepper and garnish with coriander leaves. Serve immediately.

Variation: This soup also works well using shelled uncooked prawns. Simply substitute them for the chicken and cook in the same way. Add a handful of spinach leaves at the end.

This is a great after-work summer salad that could also be served as an accompaniment to barbecued chicken or lamb. Marinate the cheese for as long as you like – it will keep in the fridge overnight.

Keep the tomatoes out of the fridge as they taste much better and sweeter at room temperature; also make sure you choose ripe tomatoes and ripe, ready-to-eat avocado.

150 g feta cheese, cut into cubes

1 garlic clove, crushed

2 tablespoons chopped fresh dill

2 tablespoons chopped fresh mint

4 tablespoons extra virgin olive oil

finely grated zest of 1 unwaxed lemon and freshly squeezed juice of ½ a lemon

freshly ground black pepper

warm crusty bread, to serve

For the salad

1 small, crisp lettuce, roughly chopped

185 g ripe plum tomatoes, cut into chunks

185 g cucumber, peeled, deseeded and roughly chopped

50 g black 'kalamata' olives, stoned

1 small red onion, peeled, stoned and thinly sliced

1 ripe avocado, peeled and cut into chunks

Serves 2

lemon and herb feta
with tomato and olive salad

Put the feta cubes in a shallow bowl. In another small bowl mix together the garlic, herbs, olive oil, lemon zest and lemon juice. Season the dressing with pepper and pour over the feta. Cover and leave to marinate for a few minutes in a cool place, or in a refrigerator for longer.

Arrange the salad leaves in 2 bowls or on 2 plates. Put the tomatoes, cucumber, olives, onion and avocado on the top, then spoon the marinated feta over the salad. Drizzle any remaining dressing over the salad and serve with warm crusty bread.

Pomegranate molasses is a thick, sticky liquiid made from reduced pomegranate juice that is used in Middle Eastern cooking. You can buy it from Middle Eastern grocers or some 'special selection' sections of supermarkets. It instantly lifts the flavour of summer fruits, duck breasts and chicken, and is a well-kept secret of many professional kitchens. If you can't get hold of pomegranate molasses, use a good, thick, syrupy balsamic vinegar or reduce a thinner vinegar slowly in a small pan until it has halved in volume.

beetroot, walnut and warm goats' cheese salad

2 tablespoons pomegranate molasses or balsamic vinegar

1 tablespoon walnut oil

freshly squeezed juice of 1 orange

1 garlic clove, crushed

200 g cooked fresh beetroot (not pickled), quartered

4 thick slices ciabatta bread

100 g firm goats' cheese, crumbled

100 g mixed salad leaves

50 g walnut halves

Serves 2

To make the dressing, mix together the pomegranate molasses or balsamic vinegar, walnut oil, orange juice and garlic in a bowl, pour over the beetroot. Cover and leave to marinate in a cool place for 20 minutes.

Meanwhile, preheat the grill to medium. Lightly toast one side of the ciabatta bread under the grill. Turn the bread over and arrange the goats' cheese on the other side. Grill for a further 3–4 minutes, or until the top begins to turn golden.

Divide the salad leaves and walnuts between 2 plates, top with the marinated beetroot and goats' cheese toasts and pour over the remaining dressing.

This combination of baby spinach, crunchy croûtes, blue cheese, grapes and pears is a sensation. Look out for the traditional French bread called ficelle, which has a hard, dark brown crust and many large air pockets. It makes delicious toasts but, if you can't find it, Italian ciabatta is more readily available and works well.

pear, blue cheese and croûtes salad

For the croûtes

100 g ficelle French bread or ciabatta

2 tablespoons extra virgin olive oil

sea salt and freshly ground black pepper

a few fresh rosemary and thyme sprigs

For the salad

2 tablespoons Sweet Mustard Dressing (see page 142)

100 g baby spinach leaves

50 g Roquefort, Stilton or other firm blue cheese, crumbled

50 g red seedless grapes, halved

1 ripe pear, cored and sliced

a baking tray

Serves 2

Preheat the oven to 200°F (400°C) Gas 6.

First make the croûtes. Cut the bread into thin slices and place them on a baking tray. Drizzle with the olive oil and sprinkle with salt and pepper to taste, and with the rosemary and thyme.

Place the baking tray in the preheated oven and cook the croûtes for about 10 minutes, or until the bread is toasted.

Pour the mustard dressing into a large bowl, add the spinach, cheese, grapes and pear and toss lightly. Pile the dressed salad into serving bowls and top with the croûtes. (You can keep any leftover croûtes in an airtight container for up to 2 weeks. Simply refresh in a warm oven before using.)

Variation: You can make this salad more substantial by adding an avocado cut into chunks, or a few tablespoonfuls of toasted pine nuts.

It is desirable to use only the crunchiest leaves in this salad, but you could, for a change, add some peppery wild rocket leaves. The salmon has been coated in a ready-made Cajun seasoning, found in the spice section of most supermarkets.

blackened salmon salad

1 garlic clove, halved

3 tablespoons olive oil

2 thick slices of ciabatta, cut into cubes

2 tablespoons Cajun seasoning

1 teaspoon sea salt flakes

2 skinless salmon fillets (each weighing about 150 g)

2 Little Gem lettuce or 1 cos lettuce, shredded

Parmesan cheese shavings, to serve

For the dressing

1 clove garlic, crushed

750 ml good-quality mayonnaise

5 anchovy fillets, finely chopped

freshly ground black pepper

Serves 2

Put the garlic clove halves in a heavy-based frying pan with 2 tablespoons of the olive oil. Heat, then add the bread cubes. Toast over medium heat, tossing frequently, until the cubes are evenly golden brown. Tip them onto a sheet of kitchen paper, discard the garlic and set aside. Wipe the pan clean.

Meanwhile, to make the dressing, put the crushed garlic in the bowl of a food processor or blender along with the mayonnaise and anchovy fillets and process until smooth. Add a few drops of hot water to thin the dressing so that it is the consistency of double cream. Season to taste with black pepper.

Mix together the Cajun seasoning and salt onto a plate and roll the salmon fillets in the seasoning mix until evenly covered. Place the clean frying pan over high heat and add the remaining oil. When the pan is smoking, add the salmon and cook for 2–3 minutes on each side until just cooked. Remove from heat and break into rough pieces.

Pour the dressing into a large bowl. Add the shredded salad leaves and toss well to coat. Arrange the dressed leaves on serving plates. Top with the blackened salmon pieces, garlic croutons and a sprinkling of Parmesan cheese shavings. Serve immediately.

Here is a tangy chicken salad that can be enjoyed as a light supper or as part of a larger meal. Pick up a rotisserie-cooked chicken on your way home from work and use the freshly roasted warm meat in this unusual and delicious Thai-style salad. The quantities will stretch to make four smaller portions or two more generous ones.

coconut thai chicken salad

900-g rotisserie-cooked chicken, preferably still warm

200 ml tinned coconut milk

2 tablespoons sweet chilli dipping sauce

4 teaspoons Thai fish sauce

freshly squeezed juice of 1 lime

For the salad

1 carrot, peeled and cut into sticks

50 g radishes, thinly sliced

1 red pepper, cored, deseeded and thinly sliced

3 spring onions, thinly sliced

1 cos lettuce, torn into bite-sized pieces

2 tablespoons roasted peanuts or cashew nuts, roughly chopped

a handful of fresh mint leaves

1 lime, quartered

Serves 2–4

Remove the flesh from the roast chicken carcass, including the wings and the legs. Tear the flesh into bite-sized pieces.

Pour the coconut milk, sweet chilli sauce, fish sauce and lime juice into a bowl and mix well using a fork. Add the chicken meat to the bowl and toss it gently in the coconut dressing until coated.

Put the carrot, radishes, red peppers, spring onions and lettuce in a bowl and toss to mix, then divide this mixture between serving plates. Arrange the coconut chicken pieces on top and spoon any remaining dressing over the top.

Sprinkle the salads with the chopped peanuts or cashew nuts, garnish with mint leaves and offer lime quarters for squeezing over. Serve immediately.

Variation: If you want to make the salad more substantial, you can add rice noodles. Place 150 g rice noodles in a large heatproof bowl, cover with boiling water and leave to sit for 3–5 minutes until just tender before draining in a colander. Toss these with the chicken and coconut dressing and serve on top of the salad.

This is a more sophisticated version of mushrooms on toast. The robust and intense flavour of the flat mushrooms with their lovely meaty juices soaking into thick, crusty toast makes a wonderful weekday supper. Use the Italian salt-cured bacon called pancetta, if you can find it. If you can't, use bacon lardons – little stubby strips of bacon. Lardons are another helpful time-saver and involve no wastage.

warm mushroom, bacon and rocket salad

1 tablespoon olive oil

4 rashers of pancetta, roughly chopped, or 50 g bacon lardons

4 medium flat mushrooms (each weighing about 75 g), left whole

1 red onion, chopped into petals

1 garlic clove, crushed

1 tablespoon red wine or cider vinegar

1 teaspoon muscovado sugar

sea salt and freshly ground black pepper

1 teaspoon wholegrain mustard

4 thick slices of Italian bread, such as ciabatta

75 g wild rocket

a drizzle of extra virgin olive oil

freshly grated Parmesan cheese, to serve

Serves 2

Heat the olive oil in a frying pan and add the pancetta or bacon lardons. Stir-fry until golden and crispy. Remove from the pan with a slotted spoon and set aside on kitchen paper, leaving the oil and fat in the pan.

Add the whole mushrooms to the pan along with the onion and garlic, cover and cook over a moderate heat for about 2 minutes on each side, or until the mushrooms begin to flatten. Take the lid off and add the vinegar, sugar, salt and pepper, mustard and 50 ml water. Cook until the sugar has dissolved. Return the pancetta or bacon lardons to the pan and keep warm.

Lightly toast the bread. Put 2 slices on each serving plate. Arrange the rocket leaves on top and drizzle with a little extra virgin olive oil. Place a mushroom on each bed of rocket and spoon the bacon and onion mixture with its pan juices over the top. Sprinkle generously with grated Parmesan cheese and serve immediately.

supper for friends
impressive yet simple dishes

Your week-night guests will be delighted with these homemade tartlets. The pastry can be cooked ahead of time and the topping added at the last moment. Ready-rolled puff pastry is a great help for cooks with little time to spare. Fresh shavings of Parmesan are best, but Parmesan shavings can also be bought in tubs – another time-saver.

roast plum tomato, goats' cheese and rocket tartlets

2 x 375-g packets of ready-rolled puff pastry, defrosted if frozen

2 tablespoons extra virgin olive oil

2 tablespoons tomato purée

a handful of fresh basil, chopped

6 ripe plum tomatoes

100 g firm goats' cheese, crumbled

sea salt and freshly ground black pepper

1 teaspoon caster sugar

40 g wild rocket or watercress

25 g Parmesan cheese, freshly shaved

2 heavy-based baking trays

Serves 4

Preheat the oven to 220°C (425°F) Gas 7.

Lightly flour a work surface. Lay out the pastry and cut it into 4 15-cm rounds using a small plate as a guide. Prick all over vigorously with a fork and place on a baking tray. Cover with baking parchment and then another heavy-based baking tray. Bake in the preheated oven for about 15–20 minutes until golden brown. Cooking the pastry this way will ensure that it does not puff up too much but remains crisp. Remove from the oven and set aside.

Preheat the grill to high. Mix together the olive oil, tomato purée and chopped basil. Spread this mixture over the cooked pastry rounds right to the edge. If you have time, peel the tomatoes. To do this, stab a tomato onto the prongs of a fork and plunge into a pan of boiling water, count to 6, then plunge straight into a bowl of cold water to stop the cooking process. The skins should just slip off easily (if the tomatoes are ripe), but if they don't, simply repeat the process.

Slice the tomatoes finely and arrange them on top of the cooked pastry rounds, making sure they overlap and reach the edges, otherwise the pastry edges will burn. Scatter the cheese over the top, season with salt and pepper and sprinkle over the caster sugar.

Put the tarts on a baking tray and place under the preheated grill to cook until the cheese begins to melt and bubble. Transfer to warmed serving plates and top each tart with some rocket leaves or watercress and Parmesan cheese shavings. Serve immediately.

Variation: You can use other cheeses, such as crumbled Greek feta, sliced mozzarella, cubed Roquefort or grated Cheddar.

The use of vodka as the poaching liquid transforms this simple salmon dish into a distinctive main course that's ideal for serving to friends. Marinating the fish in the vodka and lime for a full 10 minutes before cooking gives it a lovely citrus flavour.

vodka poached salmon with coriander pesto

100 ml vodka

finely grated zest and freshly squeezed juice of 2 limes

4 skinless salmon fillets (each weighing about 225 g)

sea salt and freshly ground black pepper

steamed, buttered green beans and mashed potatoes, to serve

For the coriander pesto

75 g pine nuts, toasted

a large bunch of fresh coriander

1 red chilli, deseeded and roughly chopped

2 garlic cloves

100 ml extra virgin olive oil

75 g Parmesan cheese, finely, freshly grated

3 tablespoons good-quality mayonnaise

Serves 4

Preheat the oven to 190°C (375°F) Gas 5.

Pour the vodka into a shallow, non-metallic ovenproof dish and add the lime zest and juice. Put the salmon fillets in the vodka mixture, season well with salt and pepper. Cover and set aside to marinate in a cool place for at least 10 minutes.

Meanwhile, make the coriander pesto. Put the pine nuts, coriander, chilli and garlic in the bowl of a food processor. Blitz until evenly chopped, then add the olive oil in a thin stream with the motor running until smooth. Transfer to a bowl and stir in the grated Parmesan cheese and mayonnaise.

Cover the salmon with foil and bake in the preheated oven for 6–7 minutes, or until just tender. Remove the salmon from the oven and discard the poaching liquid. Arrange the salmon fillets on a mound of steamed green beans with some creamy mashed potatoes and spoon a little of the coriander pesto over the top. Serve immediately.

The salsa verde that accompanies this tuna steak requires a bit of chopping, but gives the meaty fish a wonderfully intense flavour. You can prepare the potato salad ahead of time and leave it in the dressing, and the salsa verde will keep in the fridge overnight, so all you will need to do at the last minute is to cook the tuna.

tuna steak with warm potato salad and salsa verde

2 tablespoons extra virgin olive oil, plus extra to serve

4 fresh tuna steaks (each weighing about 150 g)

sea salt and freshly ground black pepper

a few fresh spinach leaves, to serve

For the potato salad

300 g baby new potatoes, scrubbed

100 ml extra virgin olive oil

freshly squeezed juice of 1 lemon

2 teaspoons wholegrain mustard

2 teaspoons chopped fresh chives

sea salt

For the salsa verde

50 g fresh flat-leaf parsley, chopped

2 tablespoons capers, drained, rinsed and chopped

4 anchovy fillets, soaked in milk, drained and finely chopped

3 garlic cloves, crushed

25 g green olives, pitted and chopped

80 ml extra virgin olive oil

freshly ground black pepper (optional)

Serves 4–6

First make the potato salad. Cook the potatoes in a pan of boiling salted water until they are just tender – about 15–20 minutes. Meanwhile, pour the olive oil into a medium bowl and add the lemon juice, mustard and chives. Whisk to form a dressing.

Drain the cooked potatoes and wait until they are cool enough to handle before cutting them into thick slices (or halves if they are very small). Toss them in the dressing until they are thoroughly coated. Set aside.

Combine all the ingredients for the salsa verde in a small bowl and mix well. Taste for seasoning and add a little pepper if needed.

Brush the olive oil over the tuna steaks and season well with salt and pepper. Heat a non-stick frying pan over a high heat, add and cook the tuna for 2 minutes on each side, turning only once.

Remove from the pan and cut each tuna steak into smaller pieces. Arrange the warm potato salad on each plate and top with the tuna. Spoon the salsa verde over the top. Serve with spinach leaves dressed with a drizzle of extra virgin olive oil.

The accompaniments for this dish need to be cooked in the right order. Start by getting the potatoes cooking, then arrange the trout on a baking tray and prepare the butter sauce. Next cook the onions for the peas and lettuce. When the potatoes are almost cooked, put the trout under the grill and finish cooking the peas.

grilled rainbow trout fillets
with mustard and caper butter

4 fresh trout fillets (each weighing about 150 g)

1 tablespoon olive oil

sea salt and freshly ground black pepper

75 g unsalted butter

freshly squeezed juice of 1 lemon

1 tablespoon small capers, drained and rinsed

1 tablespoon wholegrain mustard

a bunch of fresh tarragon, chopped

For the pan-fried potatoes

900 g new potatoes, scrubbed and halved if large

2 tablespoons olive oil

25 g unsalted butter (optional)

2 garlic cloves, thinly sliced

For the braised peas and lettuce

25 g unsalted butter

1 onion, finely chopped

2 tablespoons white wine

3 tablespoons crème fraîche

245 g frozen petits pois

1 cos lettuce, shredded

a baking tray

Serves 4

Preheat the grill to medium. Lay the fish on a lightly-oiled baking tray, skin-side down. Drizzle with the olive oil and season with salt and pepper.

To make the herb butter, melt the butter in a small saucepan over low heat and add the lemon juice, capers and mustard. Mix to combine and set aside.

Place the fish under the grill for about 4 minutes. Carefully remove from the baking tray and arrange on warmed plates. Add the chopped tarragon to the butter sauce (at the last moment so that it keeps its vibrant green colour) and immediately pour over the trout. Serve with Braised Peas and Lettuce and Pan-fried New Potatoes (see below).

Pan-fried new potatoes Cook the potatoes in a large pan of boiling salted water for about 10 minutes, or until they are just tender. Drain well.

Heat the oil with the butter (if using; it gives the potatoes a better flavour) in a large frying pan and add the hot potatoes. Sauté them over a medium heat, turning frequently until they are evenly golden brown, about 10–15 minutes. Toss the garlic in for the last 2 minutes of cooking. Drain on kitchen paper, season with salt and serve whilst hot and crispy.

Braised peas and lettuce This is a version of the classic peas *à la Française*. They are a delicious accompaniment to most fish dishes or roast chicken.

Melt the butter in a pan and cook the onion for 2–3 minutes until softened but not coloured. Add the white wine and let bubble until the liquid has evaporated. Add the crème fraîche and seasoning. Add the peas and lettuce, and allow to cook for 2–3 minutes until the peas are tender and the cos has wilted. Serve immediately.

This fast, flavoursome supper is ideal for serving to friends as a light main course. If you want to reduce preparation time further, you can use two 350-g packs of any prepared stir-fry vegetables – such as red peppers, bean sprouts and courgettes – instead of the leeks, carrots and onion.

Spiced Sweet Potato Chips (see page 64) are a perfect accompaniment. Prepare and cook these first, before you start making the scallop dish, so they will be ready when you are about to serve the scallops, which need to be eaten immediately.

chilli scallops with leeks and lime crème fraîche

2 tablespoons sunflower oil

50 g bacon lardons

2 large leeks, trimmed and cut into strips

100 g carrots, peeled and cut into strips

1 large onion, thinly sliced

2 red chillies, deseeded and finely chopped

2 garlic cloves, crushed

2 tablespoons runny honey

2 tablespoons soy sauce

16 large scallops, prepared with coral attached

sea salt and freshly ground black pepper

Spiced Sweet Potato Chips (see page 64), to serve

For the lime crème fraîche

175 ml crème fraîche

2 tablespoons chopped fresh coriander, plus extra sprigs to garnish

finely grated zest of 1 lime

1 tablespoon freshly squeezed lime juice

large non-stick frying pan or wok

Serves 4

First make the lime crème fraiche. Put the crème fraîche in a small bowl, add the chopped coriander and grated lime zest and juice and season with salt and pepper. Set aside.

Heat 1 tablespoon of the oil in a large non-stick frying pan or wok and stir-fry the bacon lardons until golden. Remove from the pan with a slotted spoon, drain and set aside on kitchen paper. In the remaining fat stir-fry the leeks, carrots, onion, chillies and garlic until soft and golden brown. Add the honey and soy sauce, transfer to a bowl or plate and keep warm.

Rinse the pan under running water and wipe dry. Add the remaining oil and heat until scorching hot. Season the scallops with pepper and fry briefly on both sides in the pan, allowing around 1½ minutes on each side; they should be firm-textured after cooking. Remove from the pan once they are cooked and keep warm.

Return the vegetable mixture and bacon lardons to the pan and reheat until piping hot. Divide the vegetables between 4 serving plates, top with 4 scallops per plate and add a generous spoonful of the lime crème fraîche. Garnish each with a coriander sprig and serve immediately with Spiced Sweet Potato Chips, if desired.

This stunning dish can be prepared even more quickly by using 2 tablespoons of red Thai curry paste instead of the lemongrass, chilli and garlic.

Follow the lead of Belgium – renowned for its Moules Frites – and serve the mussels with chips. They make a perfect partnership, along with a glass of cold beer. You can use ready-made oven chips, but I would recommend using one of the organic brands.

When serving, put a few large empty bowls on the table for used shells and offer chunks of French bread for mopping up all the delicious juices.

mussels cooked in a creamy lemongrass and lime broth

285 ml double cream

2 garlic cloves, crushed

2 red chillies, deseeded and finely chopped

1 large onion, finely chopped

2 lemongrass stalks, white part only, finely chopped

1 tablespoon Thai fish sauce

2 kg live mussels, scrubbed and beards removed (throw away any mussels that are open or float to the top in a bowl of water)

freshly squeezed juice of 1 lime

a handful of fresh basil leaves, torn

a few fresh coriander sprigs, to garnish

chips and crusty bread, to serve

Serves 4

Pour the cream into a large pan that has a tight-fitting lid and add the garlic, chillies, onion, lemongrass and fish sauce. Bring to the boil and let bubble over medium heat for about 8 minutes, or until the onions are soft.

Throw the cleaned mussels into the pan and cover. Cook, gently shaking the pan, for 2 minutes. Uncover and discard any unopened mussels at this stage. Add the lime juice and basil and stir through.

Transfer the cooked mussels to 4 warmed, deep serving bowls and spoon over any remaining sauce. Garnish each one with a fresh coriander sprig and serve immediately, with chips and plenty of crusty bread.

Serve these scrumptious chicken morsels with a simple tomato and basil salad garnished with black kalamata olives and fresh lemon wedges. It is worth making a double quantity of the goujons and freezing a batch to use another time. Once they have been coated in breadcrumbs, simply open-freeze them on baking trays, then gather them up into freezer bags. They can be cooked in the oven from frozen for about 15–20 minutes at 200°C (400°F) Gas 6.

If you can't find tarragon for the aioli, other green leaf herbs like coriander or parsley would do very well.

parmesan chicken goujons
with garlic and tarragon aioli

100 g Italian bread, such as ciabatta, roughly chopped

50 g Parmesan cheese, finely, freshly grated

freshly ground black pepper

7 tablespoons good-quality mayonnaise

3 boneless skinless chicken breasts (each weighing about 150 g), cut into strips

butter, for greasing

tomato salad and roasted new potatoes, to serve

For the garlic and tarragon aioli

1 garlic clove, crushed

1 tablespoon chopped fresh tarragon

1 tablespoon extra virgin olive oil

Serves 4

Preheat the grill to medium or the oven to 200°C (400°F) Gas 6.

Put the bread in a food processor and blitz to make breadcrumbs. Tip out onto a large plate, mix in the grated Parmesan cheese and season with black pepper.

Put 3 tablespoons of the mayonnaise in a large bowl and add the chicken strips. Turn in the mayonnaise until they are evenly coated. Lift the strips out and put them on top of the breadcrumb mixture on the plate. Gently toss until each piece is evenly coated.

Meanwhile, make the garlic and tarragon aioli. Mix together the remaining mayonnaise with the garlic, tarragon and olive oil and season with pepper.

Place the goujons on a greased baking tray, evenly spaced apart. Cook under the preheated grill for 4–5 minutes on each side (make sure that the grill is not too hot or the breadcrumbs will catch). Alternatively, cook them in the preheated oven for 10–15 minutes, turning once, until golden.

When cooked, serve immediately with the tarragon and garlic aioli for dipping and a tomato salad or, for a more substantial meal, some roasted new potatoes.

The sticky chicken can be prepared ahead of time and refrigerated in a non-metallic dish (being an acidic mixture, it would react with metal). Transfer to a roasting tin just before cooking. In place of Gorgonzola, you could use milder, creamier dolcelatte in the mash.

lemon vinaigrette roasted chicken
with gorgonzola mash

2 unwaxed lemons

175 g onions, finely chopped

2 garlic cloves, halved

6 boneless corn-fed chicken breasts with skin (each weighing about 180 g)

a handful of fresh thyme sprigs

2 tablespoons balsamic vinegar

2 tablespoons sherry or cider vinegar

4 tablespoons runny honey

150 ml olive oil

sea salt and freshly ground black pepper

wilted spinach and steamed or sautéed French beans, to serve

For the gorgonzola mash

1.4 kg floury potatoes, such as King Edwards, Maris Piper or Desirée, peeled and cut into 8 pieces

3 fresh rosemary sprigs (optional)

200 ml milk, warmed

75 g unsalted butter

125 g Gorgonzola cheese, cubed

sea salt

a small roasting tin

Serves 6

Preheat the oven to 220°C (425°F) Gas 7.

Grate the zest and squeeze the juice from 1 lemon and set aside. Thinly slice the remaining lemon. Scatter the lemon slices, onions and garlic over the base of a roasting tin just large enough to hold the chicken breasts comfortably in a single layer. Place the chicken breasts on top of the lemon slices. Season well with salt and pepper and sprinkle with thyme sprigs.

Whisk together the reserved grated lemon zest and juice, vinegars, honey and olive oil in a bowl. Pour the vinaigrette over the chicken and cook in the preheated oven for 25–30 minutes, or until the chicken is cooked through.

Meanwhile, make the gorgonzola mash. Rinse the potatoes and cook them in salted boiling water with the rosemary sprigs (if using) for 12–15 minutes, or until they start to break up. Drain and mash – you could use a potato ricer or push them through a sieve with the back of a wooden spoon. Put the potato back into the pan. Stir briefly over a low heat so that any excess moisture steams away.

Beat in the warm milk and butter and season well. Stir thoroughly until you have a smooth paste and a peaking consistency – add extra milk if necessary. Gently fold in the Gorgonzola just before you are about to serve so that the cheese is beginning to melt.

Remove the chicken from the oven and then from the tin, and set it aside in a warm place. Place the tin over a medium heat and bubble the juices until syrupy.

To serve, place a large spoonful of mash on each warmed plates and put a chicken breast on the top. Spoon over the lemon juices and accompany with wilted spinach and steamed or sautéed French beans.

You can make this tantalizingly spicy chicken jalfrezi in less time than you might wait for a take-away delivery. Make sure you have a jar of chargrilled peppers for the jalfrezi part and look out for good-quality curry pastes in supermarkets; they cut the time spent grinding or mixing the spices needed for making curry. Go for a hot variety containing spices such as chilli, cumin, coriander, tamarind and turmeric. Serve with jasmine or fragrant rice and ready-cooked poppadoms.

chicken jalfrezi

3 tablespoons vegetable oil

1 onion, roughly chopped

2 garlic cloves, crushed

1 tablespoon Madras curry paste

1 tablespoon tomato purée

400-g tin chopped tomatoes
(flavoured with mixed herbs, if available)

1 teaspoon red wine vinegar

125 g chargrilled red
peppers, chopped

125 g courgettes, diced

450 g cooked chicken, cut into
bite-sized pieces

sea salt and freshly ground
black pepper

fresh coriander sprigs, to garnish

To serve

Jasmine or fragrant rice (see page 46)

ready-cooked poppadoms

Serves 6

First cook the jasmine or fragrant rice. Drain, rinse and set aside until needed.

Meanwhile, make the curry. Heat the oil in a large frying pan, reduce the heat and add the onion and garlic. Sauté over medium heat until golden. Add the curry paste and cook for 1 minute to cook off the spices.

Add the tomato purée, chopped tomatoes, vinegar and 200 ml water to the frying pan. Bring to the boil and simmer, uncovered, for 5 minutes.

Add the chargrilled red peppers and diced courgettes and cook for a further 5 minutes until the courgettes are tender. Stir in the chicken pieces and season with salt and pepper. Simmer gently for another 6–7 minutes, or until the chicken is piping hot.

Add the coriander sprigs at the last moment and serve with jasmine or fragrant rice and poppadoms.

This is a delicious combination of lamb, tomatoes, mint and butter bean purée. You can make the purée and relish ahead of time and reheat before serving, but cook the lamb chops at the last moment. Serve with a green salad or lightly steamed green vegetables such as broccoli or sugar-snap peas.

rosemary lamb chops with cherry tomato relish and warm butter bean purée

For the butter bean purée

25 g unsalted butter

1 small onion, finely chopped

2 garlic cloves, crushed

400-g tin butter beans

3 tablespoons crème fraîche

100 ml milk

sea salt and freshly ground black pepper

freshly squeezed juice of 1 lemon

2 tablespoons chopped fresh parsley

For the tomato relish

2 tablespoons extra virgin olive oil

3 garlic cloves, crushed

1 tablespoon mint sauce

1 teaspoon caster sugar

1 tablespoon balsamic vinegar

75 g cherry tomatoes, halved

For the lamb chops

8 lamb chops (weighing about 900 g in total)

freshly ground black pepper

150 g pancetta or streaky bacon, chopped

4 fresh rosemary sprigs, leaves removed

a shallow roasting tin

Serves 4

Preheat the grill to high.

Make the butter bean purée. Melt the butter in a frying pan and add the onion and garlic. Stir over a gentle heat for 2 minutes until the onion is soft. Drain the butter beans and add them to the pan with the crème fraîche and milk. Bring to the boil and let bubble for 1–2 minutes. Using a hand potato masher, lightly crush the bean mixture, so that it looks like a rough purée. Taste and season with salt and pepper and lemon juice and add the chopped parsley. Set aside in a warm place.

To make the tomato relish, whisk together the olive oil, garlic, mint sauce, sugar and vinegar in a bowl. Pour into a small saucepan and add the tomatoes. Lightly warm over low heat for 1–2 minutes.

Season the lamb chops with pepper and place them in a shallow roasting tin. Scatter the pancetta or bacon and the rosemary leaves around the chops. Place under the preheated grill and cook for 3–4 minutes on each side.

Remove the chops from the tin and leave them to rest in a warm place for 5 minutes. Tip the pancetta or bacon and rosemary with the meat juices into the tomato mixture.

To serve, spoon a tablespoon of the hot butter bean purée onto warmed serving plates and arrange 2 chops per person on the top. Spoon the warm tomato relish over the top and serve immediately.

Since your friends can help themselves and put together their own traditional fajitas, this dish is terrifically straightforward to serve. If you prefer a very spicy guacamole, add a couple of extra jalapeño chillies, deseeded and finely chopped.

stir-fried beef fajitas with guacamole and sour cream

4 small sirloin steaks, about 2.5 cm thick (each weighing about 200 g)

4 tablespoons extra virgin olive oil

1 tablespoon pimenton (Spanish oak-smoked paprika)

1 tablespoon cumin

2 ripe Haas avocados, peeled and stoned

freshly squeezed juice of 1 lime

1 small white onion, finely grated

1 large red onion, cut into petals

1 red or green pepper, cored, deseeded and thinly sliced

3 garlic cloves, cut into slivers

8–12 wheat or corn flour tortillas

sea salt and freshly ground black pepper

100 g jalapeño chillies, deseeded and chopped

a handful of wild rocket leaves

hot chilli sauce (optional), to serve

sour cream or crème fraîche, to serve

a heavy-based stove-top grill pan (optional)

Serves 4–6

Preheat the oven 170°C (325°F) Gas 3.

Remove any fat from the beef and cut it diagonally, across the grain, to create finger-length strips. Mix together 2 tablespoons of oil, the pimenton and cumin in a large bowl. Add the beef pieces and toss until evenly coated in the spiced oil. Set aside whilst you prepare the guacamole, onions and peppers.

To make the guacamole, roughly mash the avocados in a bowl, leaving some lumps, and stir in the lime juice and white onion. Set aside until needed.

Heat a heavy-based stove-top grill pan or large frying pan over a high heat with the remaining oil and stir-fry the red onion, red or green pepper and garlic for 3–4 minutes, until they start to go limp and the edges begin to char. Remove from the pan and set aside in a warm place.

Wrap the tortillas in foil and place them in the preheated oven to warm, for about 5 minutes. (Alternatively, you can follow the packet instructions for warming them in a microwave.)

Meanwhile, wipe the grill pan clean with kitchen paper. Heat until smoking hot, then drop the strips of meat into the pan over high heat, working in batches and turning them frequently. Each batch should take no more than 1–2 minutes to cook. Season the meat with salt and pepper.

To serve, arrange the beef strips, guacamole, peppers, onion, jalapeño chillies, rocket, sour cream or crème fraîche and hot chilli sauce (if using) in separate bowls. Wrap the tortillas in a cloth napkin and put them in a basket or dish (so that they don't dry out and go hard) and bring them to the table. Let everyone dig in.

Choose lean pork escalopes for this dish and trim off any excess fat. The spicy marinade, which makes the escalopes ideal for barbecuing, can also be brushed onto chicken breasts and other meats. Begin cooking the potatoes before you cook the pork, but don't add the peas and yoghurt until just before serving.

indian grilled pork escalopes
with spiced potatoes and peas

1 tablespoon Madras curry paste

2 tablespoons mango chutney

½ teaspoon ground turmeric

2 tablespoons sunflower oil

4 loin pork escalopes (each weighing about 150 g)

150 g cherry tomatoes, on the vine if available

sea salt and freshly ground black pepper

For the spiced potatoes and peas

700 g potatoes, peeled and diced

1 tablespoon sunflower oil

25 g unsalted butter

1 onion, finely chopped

1 garlic clove, crushed

1 teaspoon cumin seeds

150 g frozen petits pois

2 tablespoons Greek yoghurt

sea salt

Serves 4

First make the spiced potatoes and peas. Cook the potatoes for 10 minutes in a pan of boiling salted water. Drain in a colander. Heat 1 tablespoon of the oil and butter in a frying pan and add the onion, garlic and cumin seeds. Cook over low heat until the onions have softened. Add the potatoes and 100 ml water, and continue to cook until the potatoes are tender, about 10 minutes.

Meanwhile, preheat the grill to high. Put the curry paste, mango chutney, turmeric and 1 tablespoon of the remaining oil in a bowl and mix well with salt and pepper. Put the escalopes on a grill rack, season well and brush with half the curry mixture. Arrange the cherry tomatoes on the grill rack alongside the pork and drizzle with the remaining oil.

Cook the escalopes and tomatoes under the preheated grill for 5–6 minutes or until the pork is slightly charred. Brush the other side with the remaining curry mixture and cook for a further 5–6 minutes.

Add the peas and yoghurt to the potatoes just before you are about to serve. Bring to the boil and let bubble for 1 minute.

To serve, put a few generous spoonfuls of the spiced potatoes and peas on warmed serving plates and place a pork escalope on top along with some tomatoes, still attached to their vine if possible.

sweet things

delicious treats

quick desserts

Most evenings a bowl of fruit salad, a piece of ripe seasonal fruit or a square of chocolate is all you need to finish off your meal. But sometimes you need to treat yourself or want to spoil your partner or guests, so these speedy desserts are the solution.

★ Hot Fudge Sauce

Melt 225 g good-quality dark chocolate in a pan with 125 ml strong black coffee. Once melted, add 75 g butter, 4 tablespoons double cream and ½ teaspoon cinnamon. Scoop balls of your favourite vanilla ice cream into a dish, pour over the luscious warm sauce and dig in! If there are two of you, there will be plenty left over for another night. Cover and keep in the fridge.

★ Raspberry Banana Split

Push 100 g raspberries through a fine-meshed, non-metallic sieve and stir in 1–2 tablespoons of icing sugar to make a sauce. Peel and halve two bananas and put them on serving plates. Add 3–4 balls of good-quality vanilla or strawberry ice cream, top with a handful of fresh raspberries and drizzle with the raspberry sauce. Sprinkle with toasted and chopped nuts such as macadamias, almonds, hazelnuts or peanuts.

★ Champagne Sorbet Cup

This should be reserved for a special occasion or when you really want to impress! In martini glasses place two scoops of best-quality blackberry or mango sorbet. Sprinkle with mixed berries (such as raspberries, strawberries or blueberries) and slowly and carefully pour a little Champagne or sparkling wine into each glass. Work quickly so that each person receives a sparkling glass.

★ Ice Cream Cookie Sandwich

Mix together 25 g shredded coconut or desiccated coconut with 25 g finely chopped toasted hazelnuts or almonds and put on a small plate. Scoop 4 balls of softened vanilla fudge- or toffee whirl-flavoured ice cream onto 4 small chocolate chip cookies. Top with a second cookie and gently press down, pushing the ice cream to the edge. Roll the ice cream in the nut mixture and serve. If making for a crowd, they can be made ahead and kept in the freezer. Remove the cookie sandwiches 5 minutes before you want to eat them, to soften.

★ Easy Mango Granita

This is a refreshing and healthy end to a meal. Peel 2 large, ripe mangoes, cut away the flesh and put it in a food processo. Purée with the juice of 1 lime. Taste and add more juice if necessary. Pour into a shallow freezer-proof dish and freeze overnight. To serve, use a spoon to scrape the frozen mango into 'icicle shards' and fill chilled martini glasses. Serve as soon as possible!

★ Speedy Apricot Fool

Use 450 g bottled apricot compote and mix with 150 ml ready-made custard or crème Anglaise and 150 ml whipped double cream. Spoon into glasses and decorate with toasted nuts. You could use other fruit compotes such as rhubarb, gooseberry or cherry in the same way.

★ Strawberry and Passion Fruit Crush

Mash one punnet of strawberries with a dash of sugar, then fold in 55 g broken ready-made meringue nests and 150 ml lightly whipped cream. Spoon into sundae glasses and top with the pulp of 2 passion fruits.

★ Cheat's Chocolate 'Tartufo'

Put 2 chocolate-covered honeycomb bars in a freezer bag and bash using the end of a rolling pin until finely crushed. Scoop rich chocolate ice cream into 4 balls and roll in the crushed honeycomb crumbs. Place on baking trays covered with parchment paper and freeze for 2 hours before serving.

★ Blueberry and Lemon Parfait

Crush 75 g shortbread into fine crumbs. Mix with 2 tablespoons of melted butter. Put half of this mixture into 2 wine glasses. Mix together 2 tablespoons lemon curd with 150 ml Greek yoghurt and spoon a layer on top of the shortbread mixture. Top with half of 150 g blueberries. Repeat the layers until the glasses are full.

★ Grilled Pineapple with Vodka

Cut off the top and bottom of a large ripe pineapple and cut off the skin in long, thin strips. Use a sharp knife to remove the 'eyes'. Slice into quarters lengthways and remove the core. Lay the pineapple on a baking tray and drizzle with 90 ml lemon vodka. Season with freshly ground black pepper. Place under a hot grill for 5 minutes until golden and serve with lemon sorbet.

★ Simple Summer Berry Brûlée

Divide 125 g mixed summer berries between 2 shallow serving bowls. Mix together 50 g each crème fraîche and fromage frais with ½ teaspoon vanilla essence and spoon over the fruits. Sprinkle each with 1 tablespoon soft brown sugar. Leave in the fridge overnight. The sugar magically melts into a caramelized brûlée-style coating.

This is the ultimate in simple puddings – if you have these ingredients in your fridge, freezer and storecupboard, you will never be caught out by unexpected guests. The secret is to make sure that the summer fruits are just frozen before pouring over the hot white chocolate sauce. Look out for good-quality white chocolate, which contains cocoa butter; inferior brands will contain vegetable fat.

iced summer berries with hot white chocolate sauce

175 g good-quality white chocolate, roughly chopped

150 ml single cream

1 teaspoon lavender honey

450 g frozen mixed summer berries (such as blueberries, strawberries, raspberries, blackberries and redcurrants)

Serves 4

Remove the summer berries from the freezer 10 minutes before you want to serve them.

Put the white chocolate, cream and honey in a heatproof bowl. Fill a large pan with cold water and bring it to a simmer. Place the bowl over the pan, but make sure that the base does not touch the water. Gently heat, stirring continuously with a rubber or wooden spatula, until the chocolate is melted and you have a smooth sauce. Alternatively, you can melt the chocolate with the cream and honey in the microwave. Place them in a small bowl and microwave for a few seconds until smooth and runny. Be careful because white chocolate scorches easily, so don't overcook it.

Arrange the semi-frozen berries on individual serving plates, then pour the hot white chocolate sauce all over the berries so that the heat of the sauce begins to melt and soften them. Serve immediately.

Variation: The hot white chocolate sauce is also delicious spooned over balls of dark chocolate ice cream or poured over chopped fudge brownies and bananas.

Cranachan is a traditional Scottish dessert marrying oats, whisky, blackberries and cream. It is an easy pudding to put together and chill ahead of time if necessary. This recipe also works well with raspberries or with a mixture of blueberries, blackberries and strawberries. If fresh berries are not in season, excellent bags of frozen mixed berries are always available in the supermarkets.

If you prefer, you can substitute any fruity alcoholic liqueur – such as peach schnapps, Grand Marnier or Cointreau – for the whisky.

blackberry cranachan

50 g organic jumbo porridge oats

25 g soft brown sugar

150 g clotted cream or extra thick cream

2 tablespoons whisky, plus extra for drizzling (optional)

250 g blackberries

a baking tray

Serves 2

Preheat the grill to medium.

Mix the oats and sugar together and spread them out on a baking tray. Place the tray under the preheated grill. Cook until the sugar is caramelized, stirring the mixture from time to time. Remove from the grill and set aside to cool.

Pour the cream into a large bowl, add the whisky and stir until smooth. Loosely break up the cooled oat mixture between your fingers and add most of the crunchy oats to the cream, reserving a few tablespoons for the top.

Place some of the berries in the bottom of 2 large wine glasses. Spoon a dollop of the cream over the top and then repeat the layers of fruit and cream a second time, finishing with the remaining blackberries.

To finish, sprinkle over the reserved oat mixture and drizzle with a little more whisky, if required. Serve immediately.

This is a grown-up version of baked bananas, flavoured with warm spices and a little citrus. Bananas are best eaten and cooked when slightly green, firm and just ripe – don't use a banana for cooking if the skin has become speckled.

The rich homemade coconut ice cream is a breeze to make as it doesn't need any churning or beating during freezing. It can be made the day beforehand and frozen overnight. But, if you don't have time to make the ice cream, simply add a dash of Cointreau or coconut liqueur to some lightly whipped or thick cream.

3 cardamom pods

freshly squeezed juice of 1 orange and 1 lime

3 tablespoons soft brown sugar

6 black peppercorns

25 g unsalted butter

2 tablespoons Cointreau, rum or brandy

4 ripe bananas, peeled

For the easy coconut ice cream

2 egg yolks

50 g icing sugar

225 g mascarpone cheese

2 teaspoons real vanilla extract

2 tablespoons coconut liqueur, such as Malibu

a shallow ovenproof dish

Serves 4

boozy bananas with easy coconut ice cream

Preheat the grill to high.

Remove the cardamom seeds from the pods and crush them using a pestle and mortar (or put the seeds in a plastic bag and crush with a rolling pin). Put the pods in a pan with the orange and lime juices, brown sugar, peppercorns, butter, cointreau, rum or brandy. Warm gently over low heat until the butter has melted.

Quarter the bananas lengthways and put them in a shallow ovenproof dish with the juice mixture. Place the dish under the preheated grill until they begin to turn golden brown, about 5–7 minutes.

Serve the bananas whilst still warm with Easy Coconut Ice Cream (below).

Easy Coconut Ice Cream Put the egg yolks in a large bowl with the icing sugar. Beat with an electric whisk for about 2 minutes, or until thickened and light in colour. Whisk in the mascarpone, vanilla extract and coconut liqueur. Scrape into a freezer-proof container and freeze for at least 6 hours or overnight. Move to the fridge to soften 10 minutes before serving.

Variation: This ice cream also goes well with a tropical fruit salad made from mango, paw paw, lychees and passion fruit.

This has the same sticky toffee sauce that is traditionally used in the famous sponge pudding, but in this recipe the tartness and spiciness of the apples cuts through the sweet, buttery toffee sauce. Sticky toffee sauce is very versatile and can be served with ice cream or spooned over other baked fruit, such as bananas, pears, peaches or apricots. The apples can be prepared in the morning and popped into the oven as soon as you get home.

baked apples with dates and sticky toffee sauce

For the sticky toffee sauce

75 g unsalted butter

75 g soft dark brown sugar

5 tablespoons double cream

For the stuffed apples

50 g dried dates, roughly chopped

½ oz stem ginger in syrup, drained and finely chopped

25 g walnuts or pecan nuts, roughly chopped

4 large cooking apples, such as Bramley or Russett, cored

pouring cream or good-quality vanilla ice cream, to serve

a medium ovenproof dish or roasting tin

Serves 4

Preheat the oven to 150°C (300°F) Gas 2.

First make the sticky toffee sauce. Put the butter, sugar and cream in a pan over low heat until melted. Bring to the boil and cook for 1 minute. Remove from the heat and set aside.

Mix together the dates, ginger and walnuts or pecan nuts. Stuff half this mixture into the cored apples and stir the remainder into the toffee sauce.

Arrange the stuffed apples in an ovenproof dish or roasting tin so that they fit tightly. Pour the toffee sauce over the apples and cover the entire dish or tin with foil.

Bake in the preheated oven for 25–30 minutes, basting the apples with the sauce occasionally. Remove the dish or tin from the oven and allow the apples to cool for 2 minutes. Serve whilst still warm, with pouring cream or vanilla ice cream.

These ripe, luscious figs poached in the mellow distinctive flavour of Marsala and served with creamy ricotta cheese are hard to beat. If figs aren't available, you can use ripe peaches or plums, but they will need an extra 5–10 minutes' cooking time. Italian ricotta cheese is a fresh, soft, snowy white cheese with a mild, slightly sweet flavour. It is less rich than cream or crème fraîche, but you can use fromage frais as an alternative if you can't find it. You can cook this pudding ahead of time and either reheat it in a low oven or serve it at room temperature.

roast figs with honey and marsala

3 tablespoons lavender or Greek honey

25 g unsalted butter, melted

1 teaspoon ground cinnamon

50 ml Italian Marsala wine or sweet dessert wine

8 large, ripe figs

100 g ricotta cheese, to serve

an ovenproof dish

Serves 4

Preheat the oven to 200°C (400°F) Gas 6.

Put the honey, butter, cinnamon and Marsala or dessert wine in a small pan. Heat gently over low heat and bring to the boil. Let it bubble for 1–2 minutes, until slightly thickened.

Using a small, sharp knife, make a 1-cm deep, star-shaped cut in the top of each of the figs. Gently squeeze the bases with your fingers to open each fruit up like a flower.

Arrange the figs upright in an ovenproof dish so that they fit tightly and pour the wine mixture over each fig. Cook in the preheated oven for about 8–10 minutes, or until slightly charred on the tips and golden.

Lift the figs onto serving plates and add a large dollop of ricotta. Spoon the deliciously syrupy juices over the top. Serve immediately.

You will find that most Italians have their own versions. This quick and easy recipe is a winner when you've got friends coming over for supper straight after work, as it can be assembled in the morning and left in the fridge to improve during the day. I always keep a packet of sponge fingers in the storecupboard and a tub of mascarpone in the fridge. A strong black espresso coffee made from freshly ground beans will give you a more intense and authentic flavour, but you can use an instant coffee (made fairly strong), if preferred.

raspberry and ginger **tiramisù**

150 g raspberries

2 teaspoons caster sugar

130 g sponge fingers (savordi biscuits)

125 ml cooled, strong black coffee, such as espresso

75 ml coffee-flavoured liqueur, such as Tia Maria or Kahlúa, or a cream liquer such as Baileys

250 g mascarpone cheese

50 g icing sugar

1 teaspoon ground ginger

1 tablespoon milk

cocoa powder, for dusting

a few pinches of ground cinnamon

4 sundae dishes, martini glasses or wine glasses

Serves 4

Put the raspberries in a bowl, add the caster sugar and lightly mash with a fork. Spoon the fruit into 4 glass sundae dishes, martini glasses or large wine glasses.

Pour the coffee and coffee or cream liqueur into a small bowl and mix together. Dip both ends of the sponge fingers in the coffee mixture so that they absorb the liquid and darken in colour, then put them on top of the raspberries. Use your fingers to press the sponge down a little to fit the glass.

Put the mascarpone, icing sugar and ginger in a large bowl and beat to combine. Gradually beat in the milk to form a smooth, creamy mixture. Spoon this mixture over the sponge fingers. Dust with a little cocoa powder and sprinkle a pinch of cinnamon over each glass.

Serve immediately or refrigerate until ready to serve.

Variation: You could use amaretti biscuits instead of the sponge fingers. They give the pudding a lovely almond flavour.

These heavenly little chocolate pots are so rich and silky, you only need to serve a small amount, but if you want to serve a more generous portion, simply double the ingredients.

They are particularly delicious served with a tiny scoop of orange or strawberry sorbet on the top (use a melon baller rather than an ice-cream scoop to make these). You could also serve the pots with some strawberries or redcurrants and a little shortbread or *langue du chat* biscuits on the side. Ideally, make them the night before you are serving them as they need a few hours to set in the fridge.

quick chocolate pots

1 egg
40 g good-quality cocoa powder
40 g caster sugar
60 g unsalted butter, softened
½ teaspoon real vanilla extract
80 ml whole milk

4 espresso or demitasse cups

Serves 4

Put the egg, cocoa powder, sugar, butter and vanilla extract in a food processor or blender. Blend until smooth. Pour the milk into a small pan and gradually bring to the boil.

Add the hot milk to the ingredients in the food processor or blender and blend on high speed until smooth. Pour the mixture into 4 tiny espresso or demitasse cups. Cover with clingfilm and put in the fridge to chill until set, 4–5 hours. Remember to take them out of the fridge a good 20 minutes before you want to eat them as the chill will spoil their silky texture.

Variations: Instead of vanilla, try these other flavours, which can be added to the milk for a subtle difference; orange zest or orange flower water, rose extract or add a fresh mint sprig to the milk before bringing it to the boil and strain before adding to the other ingredients.

These very indulgent and very chocolatey individual baked sponges are self-saucing. The option of a hazelnut and chocolate topping makes them extra special and very popular with chocoholics! Serve the puddings straight from the oven as the sponge quickly absorbs the sauce.

warm chocolate puddings

For the chocolate sauce

30 g good-quality cocoa powder

175 g soft brown sugar

For the chocolate puddings

125 g plain flour

a pinch of salt

2 teaspoons baking powder

40 g good-quality cocoa powder

250 ml whole milk

75 g unsalted butter, melted

125 g caster sugar

2 free-range eggs

1 teaspoon real vanilla extract

créme fraîche, mascarpone cheese or vanilla ice cream, to serve

For the hazelnut topping (optional)

100 ml pouring cream

2 tablespoons soft brown sugar

50 g good-quality dark chocolate, finely chopped

100 g ready-made chocolate and hazelnut spread

4 x 150-ml ramekins

Serves 4

Preheat the oven to 180°C (350°F) Gas 4.

First, make the chocolate sauce. Pour 200 ml boiling water into a small saucepan, add the cocoa powder and brown sugar and lightly whisk over a low heat making sure there are no lumps and the sugar has dissolved. Transfer the batter to a jug then pour into four dishes or ramekins.

To make the puddings, sift the flour with the salt, baking powder and cocoa powder into a large bowl. Whisk in the milk, melted butter, caster sugar, eggs and vanilla extract until a thick, smooth batter forms. Transfer the batter to a jug, then pour it into 4 x 150-ml ramekins so that the mixture comes halfway up the sides. Place the ramekins on a baking tray.

Pour the chocolate sauce mixture carefully over the prepared puddings and bake in the preheated oven for 15–20 minutes; they should still be wobbly in the centre when they are ready.

Whilst the puddings are cooking, make the hazelnut topping (if using). Put the cream and brown sugar in a small saucepan and bring to the boil, then remove the pan from the heat. Add the chopped chocolate and stir until melted. Add the chocolate and hazelnut spread and stir until smooth.

Top each pudding with a dollop of créme fraîche, marscarpone or a scoop of vanilla ice cream and offer the hazelnut topping in a warm jug for pouring (if using).

Using fresh lavender in this recipe gives the shortcakes an exquisite flavour. If you can't find any, substitute a drop or two of rosewater or orange flower water. The recipe makes about 20 biscuits. They will keep in an airtight container for up to a week and are great for offering to friends who pop in for coffee. They also freeze well, so make up a batch and keep any that are left over to make a speedy and impressive dessert any time.

We have used heart-shaped cutters here, but round, star or crescent shapes would also work well.

lavender shortcake hearts
with raspberries and lemon curd cream

For the shortcake hearts

3 lavender heads, flowers removed

55 g golden icing sugar, plus extra for dusting

115 g unsalted butter, softened

100 g plain flour

50 g cornflour

For the lemon curd cream

50 g good-quality lemon curd

100 ml double cream, whipped

100 g fresh raspberries

Serves 4

Preheat the oven to 150°C (300°F) Gas 2.

To make the biscuits, put the lavender flowers and sugar in a food processor and blitz until the lavender is powdered. Add the butter and process for 1 minute. Add the flour and cornflour and process until the mixture begins to come together to form a soft dough. Wrap and chill in the fridge for 30 minutes.

Lightly flour a work surface and tip the dough out onto it. Gently knead the dough with your hands to bring it together, then roll out to a thickness of about 3 mm.

Use a heart-shaped biscuit cutter to cut out shapes – you will need 8 to serve 4 people. Place the biscuits on a baking tray lined with baking parchment and bake in the preheated oven for 10–12 minutes, or until pale golden and set. Remove from the oven and cool on a wire rack.

To make the filling, gently fold the lemon curd into the whipped cream. To assemble, place a little of the cream in the centre of a shortbread, arrange a quarter of the raspberries over the top, place a biscuit on the top at an angle and dust with icing sugar. Serve immediately.

I use sweet eating apples in this recipe as they keep their shape, unlike cooking apples which result in a rather wet and mushy cake.

If you are using the standard size of ramekin (150 ml) this recipe will serve six, but if you have the larger 235-ml capacity ramekins it will serve four. The cakes can be cooked ahead of time, but leave them in the tin and reheat them in a warm oven before turning out and serving.

upside-down apple cakes

175 g unsalted butter, plus extra for greasing

100 g soft light brown sugar

350 g dessert apples, such as Braeburn or Cox's Orange Pippin, peeled, cored and roughly chopped

finely grated zest of ½ lemon

½ teaspoon ground nutmeg

½ teaspoon ground cinnamon

20 g walnut halves

115 g caster sugar

115 g self-raising flour

1 teaspoon baking powder

2 eggs

For the ginger cream

4 tablespoons crème fraîche

2 pieces of stem ginger in syrup, drained and finely chopped

1 teaspoon of syrup from the stem ginger

6 x 150-ml or 4 x 235-ml ramekins

Serves 4–6

Preheat the oven to 180°C (350°F) Gas 4. Lightly grease 6 x 150-ml or 4 x 235-ml ramekins.

Put the brown sugar and 60 g of the butter in a heavy-based saucepan with 2 tablespoons water and heat until melted. Gradually bring to the boil and cook for about 1 minute, or until caramelized. Spoon 1 tablespoon of the caramel sauce into the base of each prepared ramekin. Set aside the remaining sauce.

Put the chopped apples, lemon zest, nutmeg, cinnamon and walnuts in a large bowl and mix to combine. Divide the mixture between the ramekins.

To make the sponge, put the remaining butter, caster sugar, flour and baking powder in the bowl of a food processor and blend for a couple of seconds before adding the eggs. Blitz for a further 10–15 seconds, then stop as soon as the mixture comes together.

Spoon the cake mixture into the ramekins. Place them on a baking tray and cook in the preheated oven for 15–20 minutes, or until the sponge bounces back when lightly touched. Meanwhile, to make the ginger cream, mix together the crème fraîche, stem ginger and ginger syrup. Remove the cakes from the oven and run a knife around the edges. Leave to sit for 5 minutes before inverting onto warmed serving plates.

To serve, gently reheat the reserved caramel sauce and spoon over the apple cakes. Serve immediately, topped with a spoonful of ginger cream.

Having a packet of ready-rolled puff pastry in the fridge or freezer is always a great standby for an instant fruit tart. You can use practically any fruit; peaches, nectarines, apricots, plums, apples, blueberries, pineapple or a mixture of berries.

Cinnamon will go with most fruits, or you could try seasoning plums with mace or apricots with nutmeg. Flaked almonds, walnuts and pecan nuts would also be good added to the fruits.

To crush sugar cubes, put them in a plastic freezer bag and lightly beat with the end of a rolling pin. They will give a delicious crunchy effect.

individual caramelized
pear and cranberry tarts

375-g sheet of ready-rolled puff pastry, defrosted if frozen

2 large ripe pears, peeled, halved and cored

25 g dried cranberries

25 g unsalted butter, chilled and diced

milk, to glaze

3 tablespoons granulated sugar or 75 g sugar cubes, crushed (see above)

1 teaspoon cinnamon

pouring cream or crème fraîche, to serve

a non-stick baking tray

Serve 4

Preheat the oven to 220°C (425°F) Gas 7. Put a non-stick baking tray in the oven to heat.

Lightly flour a work surface and unroll the pastry. Flatten it out onto the work surface and use a sharp knife or a pizza wheel to cut it into 4 squares.

Place a pear half in the centre of each pastry square and divide the dried cranberries between the squares. Scatter with the diced butter. Brush the edges with a little milk. Mix the granulated sugar or crushed sugar cubes with the cinnamon and sprinkle over the top.

Carefully slide the tarts onto the hot baking tray and return to the preheated oven to cook for about 35–40 minutes, or until the pastry is golden brown and crisp and the pears are tender. Serve whilst still warm with pouring cream or crème fraîche.

transforming
simple food
sauces and dressings

There are plenty of ready-made bottled sauces, dressings, marinades and rubs available in the supermarkets, but they are expensive and will never taste as good as their homemade equivalents.

The easy, yet imaginative, recipes in this chapter are ideal for the busy person who wants to prepare delicious food fast. Become a creative cook by understanding how a few magic ingredients can transform simple food into something that both tastes and looks amazing. Spend a little time at the weekend making up a batch of pestos and butters, store them in your fridge or freezer and you are all set to rustle up a delicious week-night supper, bursting with fresh flavours, in no time at all. All you need do is boil some pasta, grill a piece of fish or assemble a simple salad and add your magic ingredient. An invaluable piece of equipment, for most of these recipes, is a mini food processor.

homemade pestos

Homemade pesto not only looks and smells better than a pesto from a jar – it also tastes better! Pestos are perfect for stirring into cooked pasta, spreading on pizzas or using as a topping for grilled fish or chicken. Put the pestos in a screw-top jar, add a thin layer of oil and store them in the fridge for up to a week. They also freeze well.

mint, ginger and almond pesto

This is lovely spooned over grilled fish or barbecued vegetables, added to clear vegetable soup or tossed into cooked noodles. Toasting the almonds gives the pesto a more intense flavour. Look out for packets of pre-toasted almonds or toast them yourself in the oven for 5–6 minutes at 200°C (400°F) Gas 6. Keep an eye on them as they burn quickly.

2-cm fresh ginger root, peeled and grated

20 g fresh mint leaves

8 tablespoons vegetable oil

2 tablespoons light soy sauce

1 tablespoon freshly squeezed lime juice

1 garlic clove, crushed

100 g almonds, toasted

Put all the ingredients in the bowl of a mini food processor and blitz until smooth.

coriander, chilli and peanut pesto

This hot and spicy pesto is perfect with vegetable and prawn stir-fries, stirred through pasta or noodles and served as a dip for crudités.

100 g roasted and salted peanuts

1 garlic clove, crushed

1 red or green chilli, deseeded and chopped

20 g fresh coriander leaves

finely grated zest of 1 lime

100 ml groundnut or sunflower oil

sea salt and freshly ground black pepper

Put the peanuts, garlic and chilli in the bowl of a mini food processor. Blend, then add the coriander and lime zest, season generously and pulse to form a course mix. Allow the motor to run and then, in a steady flow, add the groundnut oil to form a smooth paste. Taste and season as necessary.

red pepper and walnut pesto

Serve this warm as a dip for crudités, stirred into cooked pasta, spooned over grilled halloumi cheese or as a sauce with grilled lamb or steak.

2 chargrilled red peppers

55 g walnut pieces, toasted

3 spring onions, chopped

1 garlic clove, crushed

2 tablespoons chopped fresh parsley

4–5 tablespoons extra virgin olive oil

sea salt and freshly ground black pepper

Put all the ingredients in a mini food processor and blitz until smooth. Taste and season as necessary.

Variation: If you have time, roast your own red peppers; place under a preheated high grill until the skins are blackened on all sides. Remove and put in a plastic bag for 10 minutes, then slip off the skins.

Other quick ideas for pesto:

★ Swirl a tablespoonful of pesto into vegetable soup to add extra flavour and colour.

★ Spread on a chicken or ham sandwich instead of mayonnaise.

★ Spread on a toasted English muffin and top with sliced tomatoes, a drizzle of olive oil and some freshly ground black pepper.

★ Use to perk up dressings, mayonnaise or sour cream dressing.

★ Use in place of a tomato sauce on a homemade pizza.

★ Dollop onto baked potatoes or omelettes.

★ Add a dash of pesto to tinned tomato soup to bring it back to life.

artichoke and almond pesto

This has a lovely creamy texture and subtle flavour. Add to pasta or spread onto warm ciabatta toasts, or serve as a dip with *grissini* (bread sticks). Marinated artichoke hearts can be found loose at deli counters or in jars in the Italian section of supermarkets.

4–6 roasted and marinated artichokes hearts, drained

100 g almonds, toasted

2 tablespoons chopped fresh basil

1 garlic clove, crushed

4 tablespoons extra virgin olive oil

30 g Parmesan cheese, finely, freshly grated

sea salt and freshly ground black pepper

Put the artichokes, almonds, basil and garlic in a mini food processor. Blitz until the mixture looks like coarse meal. Add the oil in a thin stream with the motor running to form a smooth paste. Transfer the purée to a bowl and stir in the Parmesan cheese. Taste and season as necessary.

broccoli, parmesan and basil pesto

This is a wonderfully vibrant green pesto and is delicious tossed through pasta, spread onto toast or served as a warm dip.

125 g broccoli florets

25 g pine nuts, toasted

1 large garlic clove, crushed

1 red chilli, deseeded and finely chopped

3 tablespoons extra virgin olive oil

55 g Parmesan cheese, finely, freshly grated

freshly squeezed juice of ½ lemon

sea salt and freshly ground black pepper

Cook the broccoli in a pan of boiling salted water until tender, about 6–7 minutes. Drain. Meanwhile, put the pine nuts, garlic and chilli in a mini food processor and pulse to form a coarse mix. Add the broccoli and olive oil and pulse until the mixture is smooth. Add the Parmesan cheese and lemon juice and pulse again. Taste and season as necessary.

classic basil pesto

A lot of precious leaves are needed to make up this sauce, but it is well worth the indulgence. Serve with pasta, spread on toasts and pizza, or add to mashed potatoes and soups.

50 g fresh basil leaves

1 large garlic clove, crushed

25 g pine nuts, toasted

5–6 tablespoons extra virgin olive oil

pinch of sea salt

25 g Parmesan or Pecorino Romano cheese, finely, freshly grated

Put the basil, garlic, pine nuts, olive oil and salt in a mini food processor. Blend until smooth, then stir in the grated cheese.

flavoured butters

Flavoured butters are quick and easy to make and can transform otherwise plain food in an instant. If you have a microwave, the butters can be softened for about 15 seconds and the flavourings beaten into the butter in a bowl. Alternatively, you can simply combine all of the ingredients in a mini food processor.

lemon and basil butter

This has a lovely fresh and zingy flavour. Melt over steamed asparagus and broccoli, or serve with baked or grilled fish. Use instead of plain butter in a smoked salmon sandwich.

125 g unsalted butter, softened
1 teaspoon finely grated lemon zest
1 tablespoon finely chopped fresh basil
freshly ground black pepper
2 tablespoons lemon juice

Put the softened butter, lemon zest and basil in a bowl and season with pepper. Beat until smooth, adding the lemon juice gradually and beating after each addition. Scoop the prepared butter out onto a large piece of greaseproof paper or clingfilm and shape into a log about 13 cm in length, wrap well and twist each end. Chill in the fridge for at least 25–30 minutes, or until firm. Cut the butter into handy 1-cm slices. Store in an airtight container in the fridge for up to 2 weeks or bag up, label and freeze for up to 1 month.

tarragon and mustard butter

This butter works well with steak, tuna or salmon, grilled chicken or duck breasts or homemade burgers. It even makes Brussels sprouts a joy! Blanching the tarragon in boiling water keeps the leaves a brilliant green and enhances the flavour, but it's not essential to do this.

3 tarragon sprigs, leaves removed
125 g unsalted butter, softened
2 tablespoons wholegrain or coarse-grain mustard
sea salt and freshly ground black pepper

Cook the tarragon leaves in a pan of boiling salted water for 2 minutes. Drain and rinse under cold running water, then dry thoroughly. Put the softened butter, blanched tarragon, mustard and pepper to taste in a bowl and beat until smooth. Follow method for chilling as for Lemon and Basil Butter (left).

moroccan spiced butter

This is a great instant butter as all the dry ingredients are likely to be in your storecupboard. It works well with grilled lamb chops, pan-fried flat mushrooms or chargrilled aubergines and courgettes. Crushing the whole spices really brings out the flavours and essential oils, but you can use ground coriander and cumin, if easier.

1 teaspoon dried chilli flakes
1 teaspoon coriander seeds
1 teaspoon cumin seeds
½ teaspoon sea salt flakes
125 g unsalted butter, softened

Put the spices and salt in a mortar and crush lightly with a pestle. Alternatively, put the spices and salt in a heavy bowl and grind using the end of a rolling pin. Beat the seasoning mix into the softened butter in a bowl until evenly combined. Follow method for chilling as for Lemon and Basil Butter (far left).

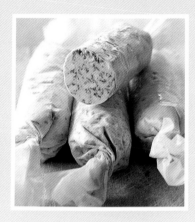

Quick ideas for flavoured butters:

★ Spread onto bread rolls, use as part of a sandwich filling or smear onto hot toast for a quick and tasty snack.

★ Add extra taste to steamed vegetables, corn-on-the-cob or baked potatoes.

★ Melt over grilled and barbecued meats or use as a seasoning on plain grilled steaks, pork chops or lamb steaks.

★ With chicken – use your fingers to push the butter under the skin of chicken breasts before oven-baking them.

★ With fish – smear over fish fillets before grilling, use to pan-fry a fillet of fish or serve melting over a bowl of mussels.

★ Add to gravies and sauces to invigorate and enrich the flavour.

gorgonzola and garlic butter

This goes magnificently with steak. Tuck slices of butter between steak halves and top with another butter slice just before serving. It also works well with pork chops or smeared under the skin of chicken breasts before baking them in the oven.

125 g unsalted butter, softened

2 garlic cloves, crushed

75 g Gorgonzola or other firm blue cheese, such as Stilton, crumbled

2 tablespoons finely chopped fresh parsley

Put the softened butter in a bowl with the garlic, blue cheese and parsley, and beat until evenly combined. Follow method for chilling as for Lemon and Basil Butter (see facing page).

anchovy and caper butter

Smother on grilled fish fillets, such as salmon, mackerel or haddock, or spread onto hot toast and top with wild rocket leaves.

2 garlic cloves, crushed

5 anchovy fillets, soaked in milk for 10 minutes and drained

2 tablespoons capers, rinsed and drained

1 tablespoon chopped fresh parsley

a squeeze of lemon juice

125 g unsalted butter, softened

freshly ground black pepper

Put the garlic, drained anchovy fillets, capers, parsley and lemon juice in the bowl of a mini food processor. Blend until smooth. Add the butter and blitz until evenly combined. Season with pepper. Follow method for chilling as for Lemon and Basil Butter (see facing page).

hot paprika butter

Spanish oak-smoked paprika (hot pimentón) is not like the relatively bland paprika spice that we are used to. It has a strong hickory-smoked flavour and is often used to season Tex-mex pork, beef and lamb casseroles. This incredibly speedy butter is delicious served with barbecued steaks or chicken breasts, or melted in a baked potato.

125 g unsalted butter, softened

2 teaspoons hot pimentón (Spanish oak-smoked paprika)

Put the softened butter in a bowl with the paprika and beat until evenly combined. Follow method for chilling as for Lemon and Basil Butter (see facing page).

marinades and spice rubs

Marinades tenderize and add flavour to meat and also add a bit of zing to fish and vegetables. Spice rubs are generally used to season raw meat and fish, but they can also be mixed with butters and oils. Make rubs in big batches as they will keep for about two months in screw-top jars, if stored in a cool, dark place.

soy, honey and chilli marinade

This spicy Thai marinade is great for tossing into prawns before grilling, or brushing onto chicken breasts before oven-baking or stirring into strips of pork before stir-frying.

2 tablespoons soy sauce

1 tablespoon runny honey

2 teaspoons Thai fish sauce

2 tablespoons sweet chilli sauce

Put all the ingredients together in a small bowl and whisk until evenly combined.

Place the food you are marinating in a shallow, non-reactive dish. Pour the marinade into the dish and turn the food once to make sure it's coated. If you can, cover and let it marinate in a cool place for about 30 minutes. When ready to cook, remove from the marinade and cook as intended.

tex-mex marinade

This is a 'hickory' marinade for spare ribs or chicken drumsticks. It's also a great sauce to serve with barbecued burgers or good-quality sausages.

2 tablespoons tomato ketchup

1 garlic clove, crushed

250 ml passata (sieved tomatoes)

1 tablespoon red wine vinegar or balsamic vinegar

1 tablespoon Worcestershire sauce

2 teaspoons Tabasco sauce

½ teaspoon pimentón (Spanish oak-smoked paprika)

2 tablespoons chopped fresh coriander

freshly squeezed juice of ½ lime

Put the ketchup, garlic, passata, vinegar, Worcestershire sauce, Tabasco, paprika and 250 ml boiling water in a pan. Cover and simmer for 10 minutes. If using as a marinade, set aside to cool. If using as a sauce, stir in the coriander and lime juice just before serving. To use, follow method for Soy, Honey and Chilli Marinade (left).

greek lemon and herb marinade

This marinade uses three classic Greek ingredients – olive oil, lemon and oregano. It can be used to marinate vegetables, meat or fish and also as a basting sauce when cooking chicken. It is lovely drizzled over grilled halloumi cheese or a feta, olive, tomato and onion salad.

finely grated zest and freshly squeezed juice of 1 lemon

1 tablespoon chopped fresh oregano

1 teaspoon freshly ground black pepper

1 teaspoon sea salt flakes

80 ml extra virgin olive oil

Put the lemon zest in a mortar or heavy bowl and add the oregano, pepper and salt. Grind with a pestle or sturdy wooden spoon to release the essential oils in the lemon and oregano. Whisk in the lemon juice and olive oil in a steady stream with a wire whisk. To use, follow method for Soy, Honey and Chilli Marinade (far left).

More easy marinades and rubs

★ **Plum and soy** Mix 4 tablespoons plum sauce with 2 tablespoons soy sauce. Good for brushing onto pork chops, spare ribs, duck breasts or chicken breasts

★ **Marmalade and ginger** Mix 4 tablespoons thick-cut marmalade with 1 tablespoon sweet chilli sauce, 1 teaspoon soy sauce and 1-cm piece of peeled and finely grated fresh ginger root to make a sticky marinade that's good with chicken breasts, duck breasts and pork and lamb chops.

★ **Chinese five spice** Mix together 2 tablespoons soy sauce, ½ teaspoon Chinese five-spice powder, ½ teaspoon runny honey, ½ teaspoon garlic powder and 2 tablespoons sesame or groundnut oil. Great for marinating fish or adding to vegetable stir-fries.

mustard and herb rub

This is good for rubbing onto pork chops or smearing onto the trimmed fat of a rack of lamb. Or try massaging into chicken fillets and steaks.

2 tablespoons Dijon mustard
1 tablespoon chopped fresh flat leaf parsley
2 teaspoons chopped fresh mint
2 teaspoons chopped fresh chives
freshly ground black pepper

Mix the mustard with the fresh herbs and season with pepper. Store in a dry screw-top jar until required.

Pat the food you're cooking dry with kitchen paper. Using your fingers, rub the outside surface of the meat or fish with the seasoning blend. If you have time let the food sit at room temperature for 15 minutes before cooking.

cajun spice rub

Great for rubbing into the skin of roast chicken or for sprinkling on lamb chops. Try this rub for the Blackened Salmon Salad (page 76).

1 teaspoon dried oregano
1 teaspoon dried thyme
1 teaspoon garlic powder
1 teaspoon pimentón (Spanish oak-smoked paprika)
1 teaspoon cayenne pepper
1 teaspoon soft light brown sugar
1 teaspoon dry English mustard powder
2 teaspoons sea salt flakes

Mix all the ingredients together in a bowl and then store in a dry screw-top jar until required. To use, follow method for Mustard and Herb Rub (left).

middle eastern rub

This spicy seasoning works well with steak, lamb chops, pork fillet, or oily fish. It can also be rubbed onto chicken skin or a shoulder of lamb before roasting, which will give the meat an intense aromatic taste. For speed, I've given ground herbs here, but you can grind whole spices.

2 tablespoons extra virgin olive oil
½ teaspoon ground ginger
½ teaspoon ground coriander
½ teaspoon ground cumin
½ teaspoon sea salt flakes
½ teaspoon cardamom pods, pods removed and seeds crushed
½ teaspoon ground cinnamon
½ teaspoon ground allspice
½ teaspoon cayenne pepper
finely grated zest of 1 orange

Mix all the ingredients together in a bowl. To use, follow method for Mustard and Herb Rub (far left).

★ salad dressings

A good salad dressing is only as good as the ingredients you use. For simple salad leaves, drizzle extra virgin olive oil, add a drop of balsamic vinegar and a sprinkling of sea salt and freshly ground black pepper to a salad bowl before you add the salad leaves. Add a few sprigs of a fresh green herb, such as coriander, basil or mint, and you've got a masterpiece of a salad without any fuss.

blue cheese dressing

This is a great dressing for using up those leftover bits of blue cheese lurking in the back of your fridge. Blue cheese goes particularly well with pears or can be used to liven up a chicken salad. Once made, the dressing will keep for up to 1 week in the fridge.

50 g firm blue cheese, such as Stilton or Roquefort
2 tablespoons sherry or cider vinegar
3 tablespoons walnut or hazelnut oil
3 tablespoons sunflower oil
1 teaspoon Worcestershire sauce
freshly squeezed lemon juice, to taste
freshly ground black pepper

Put all the ingredients, except the lemon juice, in the bowl of a food processor and process until smooth. Add a little lemon juice and pepper to taste.

caesar dressing

This is a speedy version of the popular dressing. Perfect with any green salad leaves and works well with roast chicken or avocado. Once made, the dressing will keep for up to 1 week in the fridge.

1 free-range egg
1 garlic clove, crushed
2 teaspoons Worcestershire sauce
1 teaspoon anchovy essence
1 tablespoon freshly squeezed lime juice
3 tablespoons extra virgin olive oil
25 g Parmesan cheese, coarsely, freshly grated
sea salt and freshly ground black pepper

Put the egg in a pan of cold water and bring to the boil. Boil for 1 minute and then plunge into cold water to stop the cooking process. Once the egg is cool enough to handle, crack it into a mini food processor and add the garlic, Worcestershire sauce, anchovy essence, lime juice and olive oil. Process well, then stir in the Parmesan cheese and add pepper to taste.

sweet mustard dressing

This dressing is slightly sweeter than a classic vinaigrette. It has a creamy emulsified texture and is good for drizzling over sliced tomatoes and mozzarella and works well with bitter salad leaves like chicory, rocket or frisée lettuce. If you prefer, you could use American-style yellow mustard instead of Dijon. Once made, the dressing will keep for up to 1 week in the fridge.

1 tablespoon Dijon mustard
2 teaspoons acacia or lavender honey
1 tablespoon cider vinegar
6 tablespoons extra virgin olive oil
sea salt and freshly ground black pepper

Put all the ingredients in a screw-top jar and shake vigorously until the dressing is emulsified. Add salt and pepper to taste.

Other quick salad ideas:

★ **Instant Caesar Salad** Tear 1 cos lettuce into pieces and toss it in some Quick Caeser Dressing (see facing page). Add a handful of ready-made croûtons and some pre-cooked bacon pieces and grate some Parmesan cheese over the top.

★ **Quick Saffron Potato Salad** Mix 2 tablespoons of Garlic and Saffron Aioli (see below) with 200 g cooked new potatoes.

★ **Mixed Bean Salsa** Mix the Mediterranean Salsa (see below) with a drained tin of mixed beans, 2 chopped plum tomatoes and some chopped spinach and spring onions.

★ **Quick Niçoise Salad** Mix the Herb Vinaigrette (see below) with a drained tin of tuna. Toss in some salad leaves, chopped cucumber, cherry tomatoes, sliced red onion, black olives and hard-boiled eggs.

herb vinaigrette

The sprigs of herbs and garlic used here will infuse the vinaigrette the longer they are left in the dressing. It is the most useful and versatile dressing in my kitchen. Once made, the dressing will keep for up to 1 week in the fridge.

1 tablespoon freshly squeezed lemon juice

1 tablespoon white wine vinegar or tarragon vinegar

sea salt and freshly ground black pepper

1 teaspoon caster sugar

7 tablespoons extra virgin olive oil

1 garlic clove, halved

a few fresh herb sprigs, such as tarragon, coriander or mint

Put the lemon juice, vinegar, salt, and pepper to taste, sugar and olive oil in a screw-top jar. Shake the jar vigorously until the dressing is smooth. Add the garlic halves and herb sprigs.

garlic and saffron aioli

This is delicious served with grilled or barbecued fish or chicken, or served as a dip for potato wedges. Look out for smoked garlic – it has a much less intense flavour. Once made, this dressing will keep for up to 1 week in the fridge.

150 ml good-quality mayonnaise

2 garlic cloves, crushed

a pinch of cayenne pepper

a pinch of saffron threads

1 tablespoon extra virgin olive oil

Put all the ingredients in a bowl and whisk until combined. Cover with clingfilm and chill in the fridge for about 1–2 hours, to allow the saffron flavour to develop fully. Stir well before serving.

mediterranean salsa

This is perfect for cheering up grilled or barbecued fish fillets or chicken breasts, or serving as a dip. A spoonful will also brighten up a ready-made soup. Once made, it will keep for up to 1 week in the fridge.

1 tablespoon red wine vinegar

2 tablespoons small capers, rinsed, drained and finely chopped

1 garlic clove, crushed

½ teaspoon anchovy essence

½ teaspoon Dijon mustard

2 tablespoons chopped mixed fresh herbs, such as basil, tarragon, parsley and mint

freshly squeezed juice of ½ lemon

½ small onion, finely chopped

150 ml extra virgin olive oil

freshly ground black pepper

Put the vinegar, capers, garlic, anchovy essence and mustard in a heavy-based bowl and use the end of a rolling pin to work the mixture until evenly combined. Whisk in the herbs, lemon juice, onion, olive oil and pepper, to taste.

index